THREE HUNDRED AND SIXTY-FIVE

Daily Paintings by Deborah Last

Painting Every Day for a Year

The landscape has been an enduring passion within my work and though I will often work with other subjects, I return to the landscape constantly.

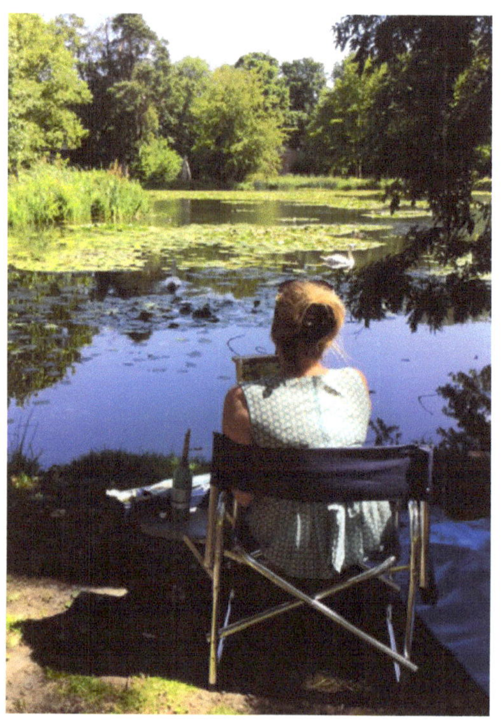

In December 2014 I began to form the idea that I would spend 2015 really grasping what the landscape means and how I might interpret what I see in a strong and unique way.

Thus began the idea of daily painting for a year. Daily painting has become quite a popular way to work and there are many artists who pursue this route. I wanted to discipline myself to work from life, en plein air, as much as possible and to really paint the day I was in. I wanted to "get out there" every day and record what I was seeing, to push my dedication to the artistic life to the max.

I painted on birthdays and on Christmas Day, at a family wedding, even on very sad family days, in memoriam.

Living as I do within the Stowe School estate meant that I had access to one of the most beautiful landscapes in the world. This landscape was very much the pull for me to even begin the year long commitment. Though there are paintings from other places as we did go away, the major body of the work is Stowe Landscape Garden.

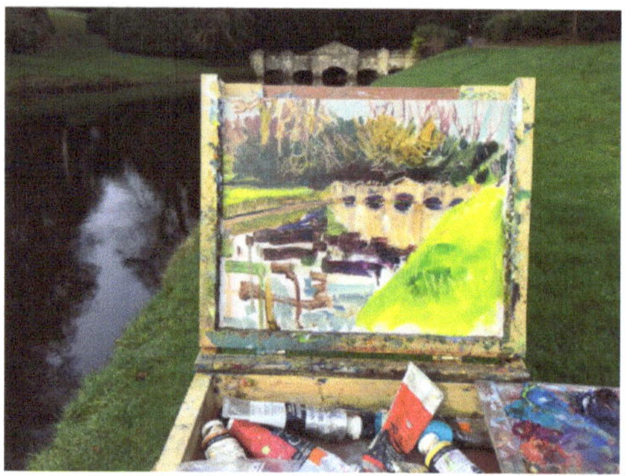

So on the 1st of January 2015 I set out, sketchbook in hand and made my first foray into this daily painting pursuit. I had already got a few days down in December and felt that this would be achievable.

Each day I quietly did my painting not really telling anyone what I was doing. I began to work out a system for recording what I was painting and where. I was painting on two sizes of board.

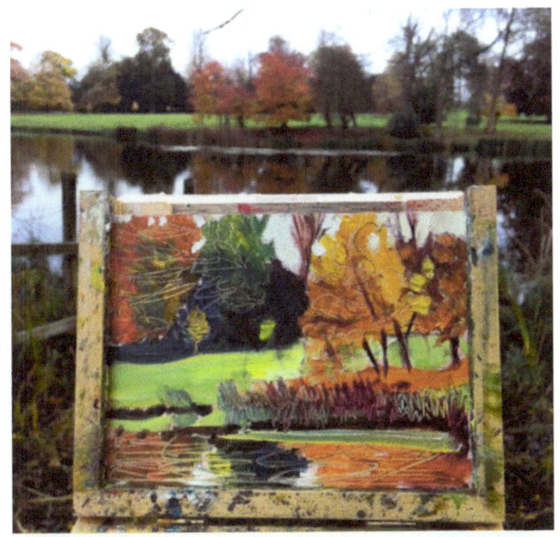

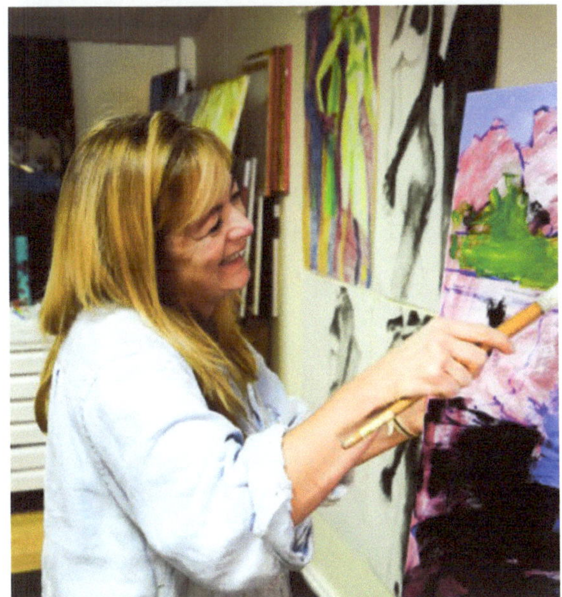

By the spring there were lots of requests for me to sell the paintings and so that also began, rather than waiting till the whole year was done. People requested special days and even booked birthdays in advance requesting special locations within the garden.

As January progressed it became obvious that I needed to photograph the paintings and it might be good to share what I was doing. With a nudge from my son, I joined the world of Instagram and sent every post to my artist page on Facebook.

Suddenly I had an accountability to the project that was not there before. People quickly seemed to pick up on it and before long I had people saying things like "I look to see your painting posted every day" and "I'm loving following them."

It certainly helped knowing there were people who were actually watching and interested!

It was an incredible journey in many ways, recording and painting holidays and family events but most of all it has informed my own artistic development.

I have developed a clearer style and introduced stronger colours, adding magenta and turquoise into the palette in September when I felt I needed to lift how the paintings were looking.

Sitting in my studio, looking at the many paintings that have developed from that year, I can truly say that I have indulged and delighted in my passion for the landscape and plan to continue to do so for many years to come.

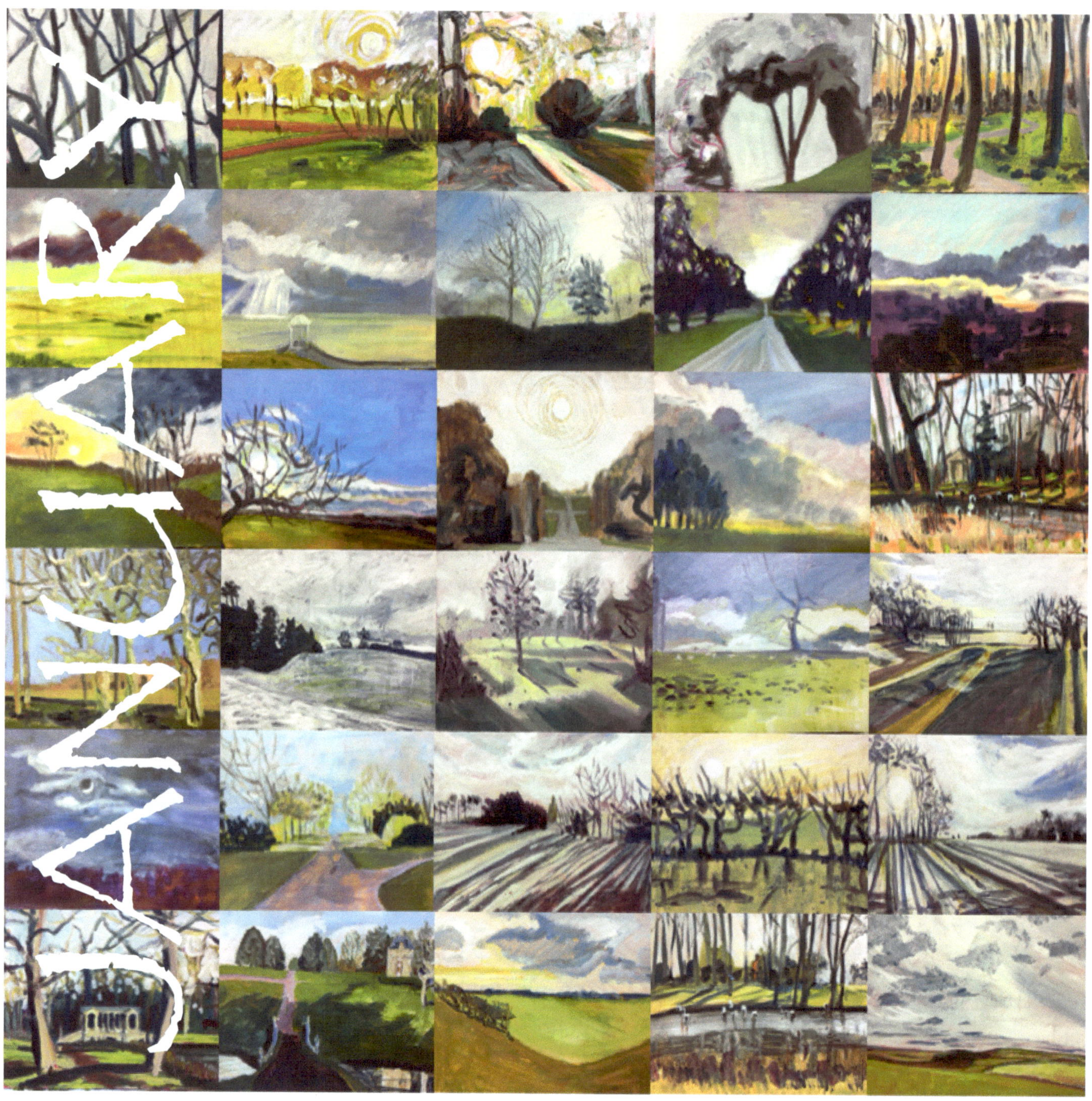
JANUARY

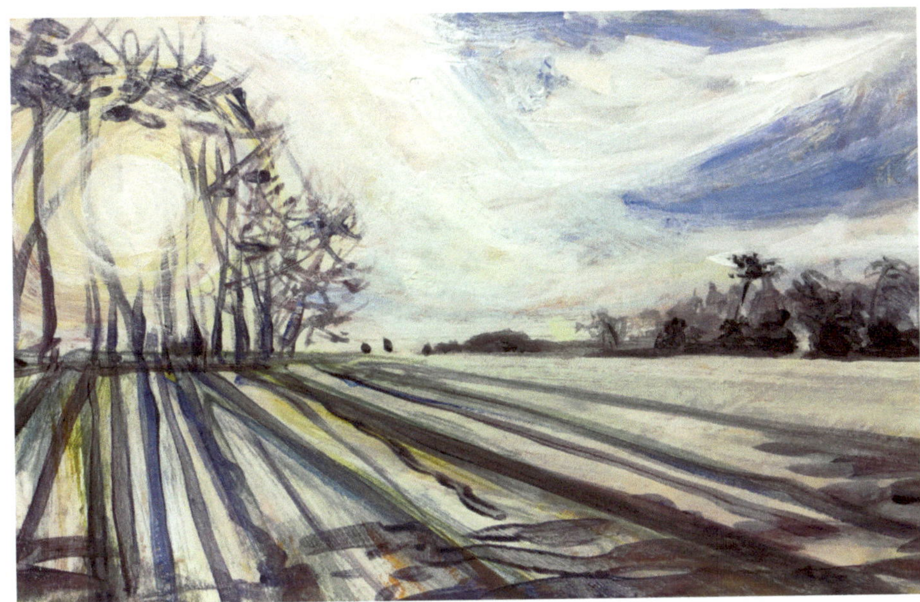

'Sunlight Through Trees'
20th January

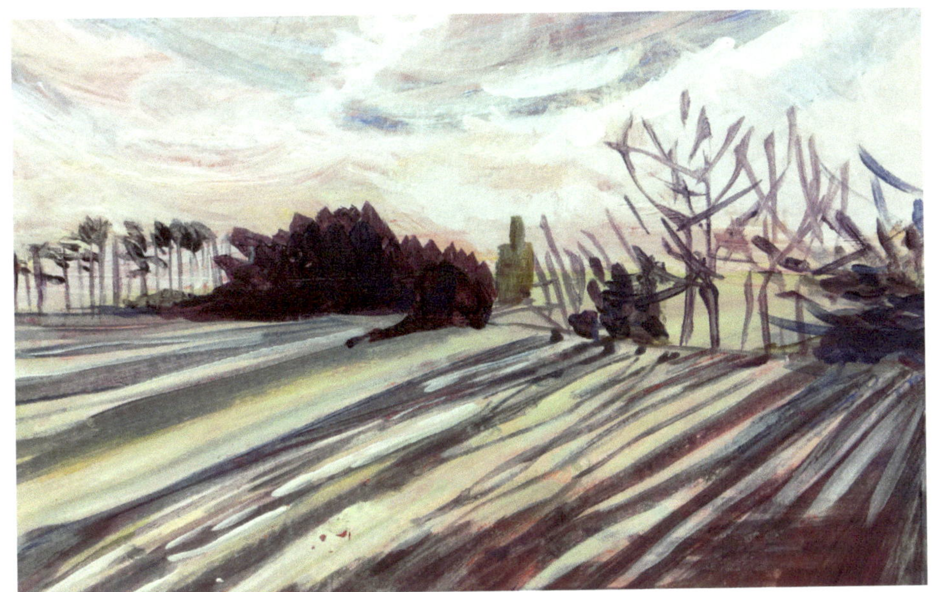

'Towards the Bourbon Tower'
21st January

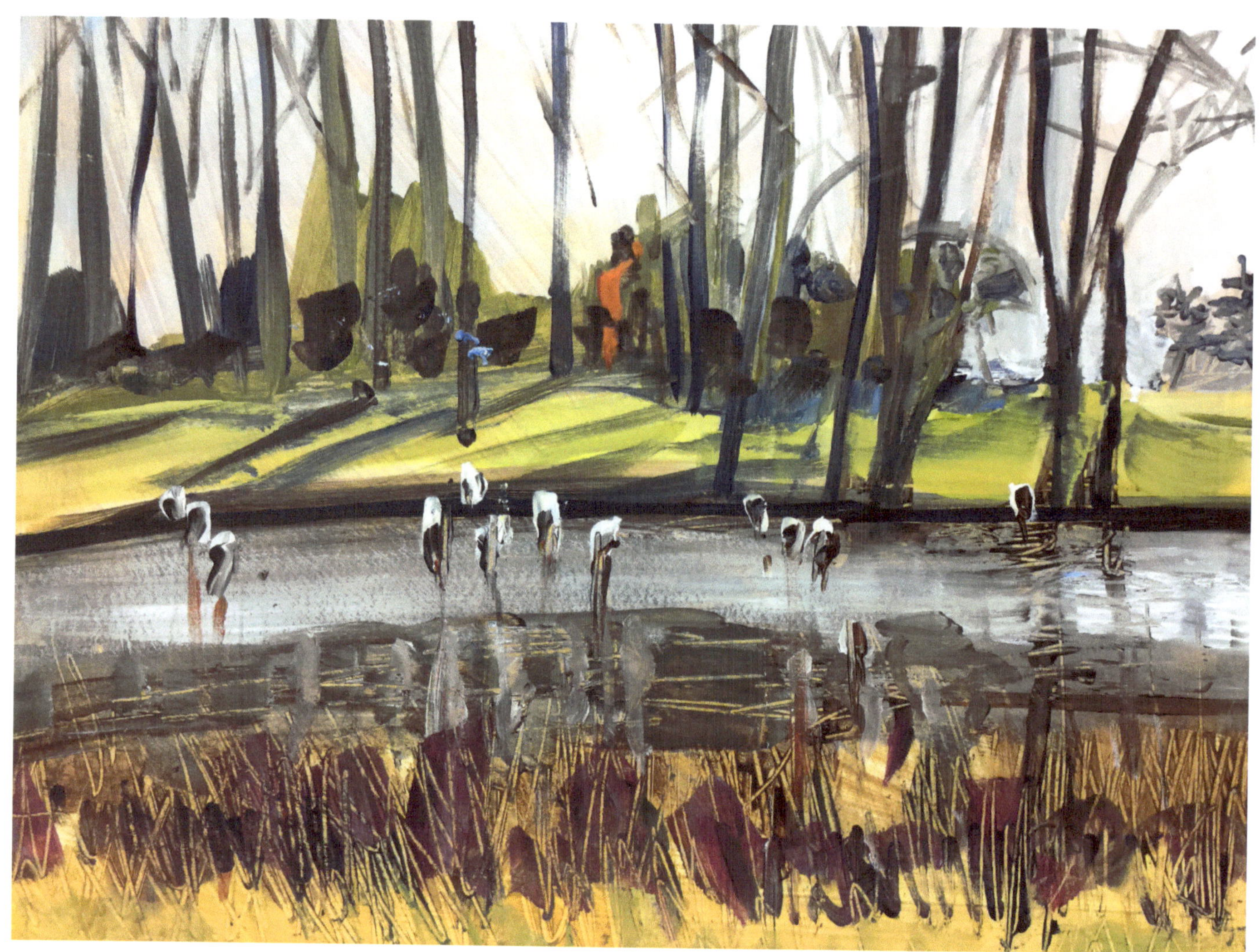

'The Octagon Lake from the Wooden Bridge'
30th January

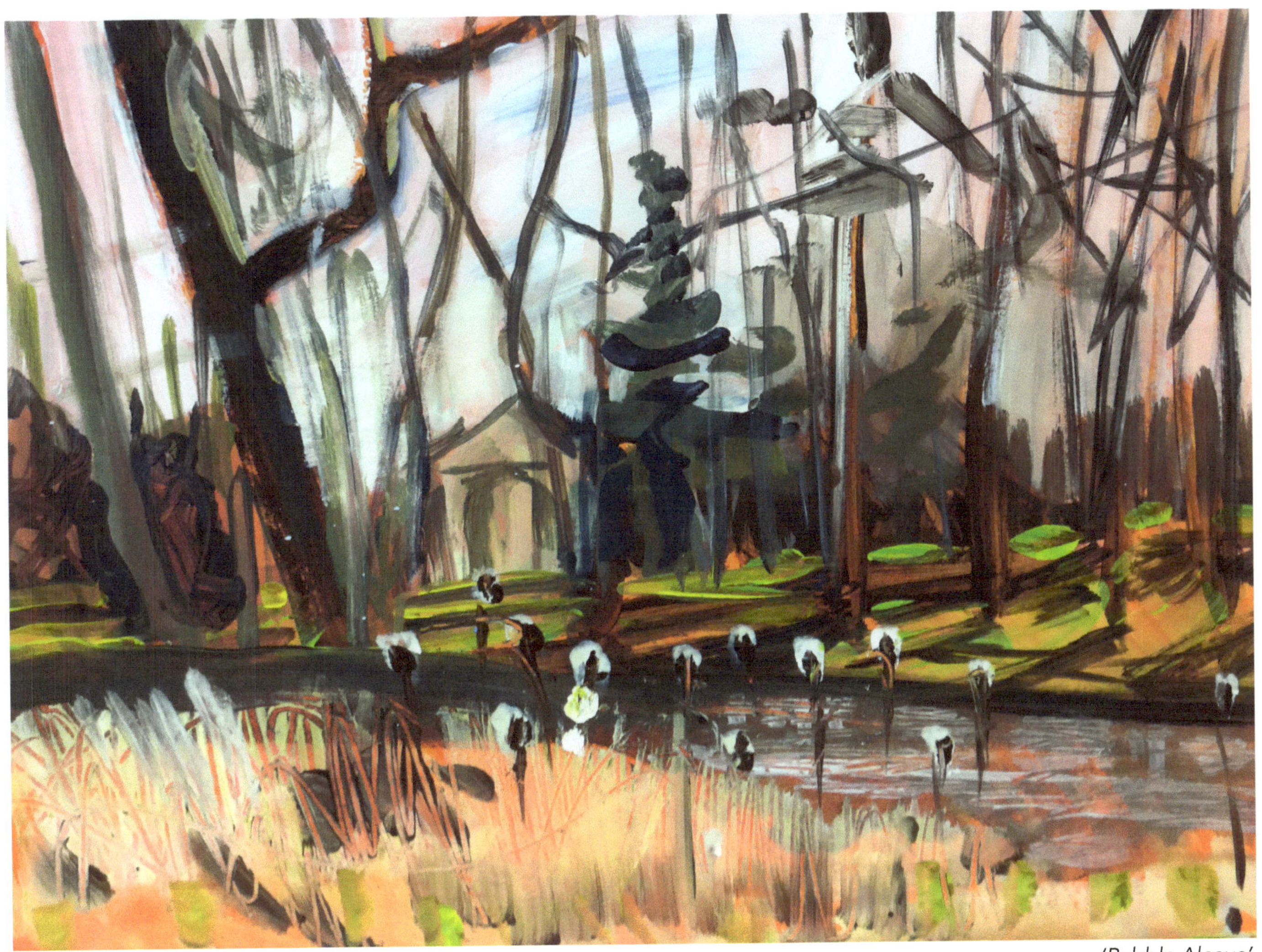

'Pebble Alcove'
31st January

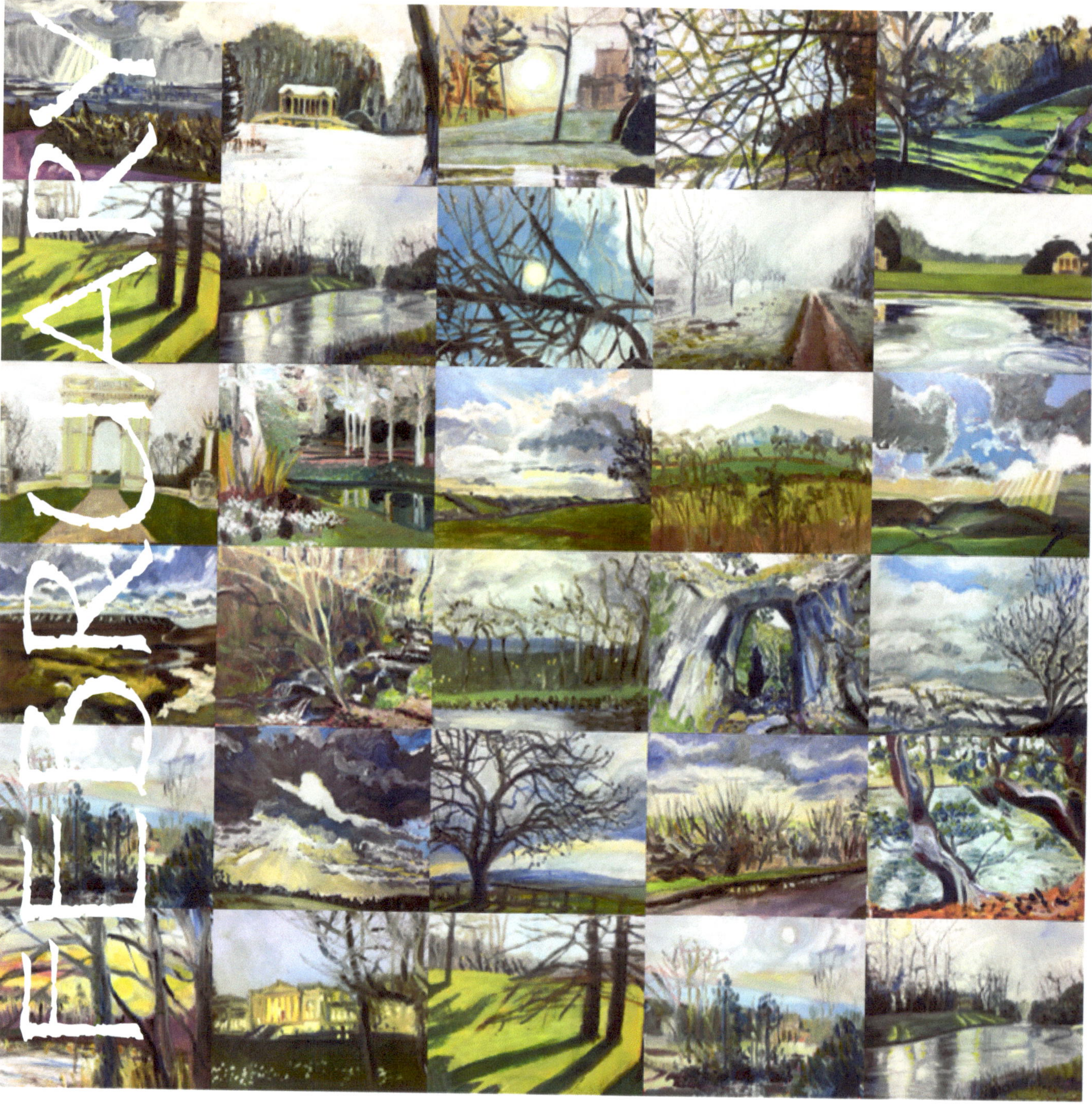
FEBRUARY

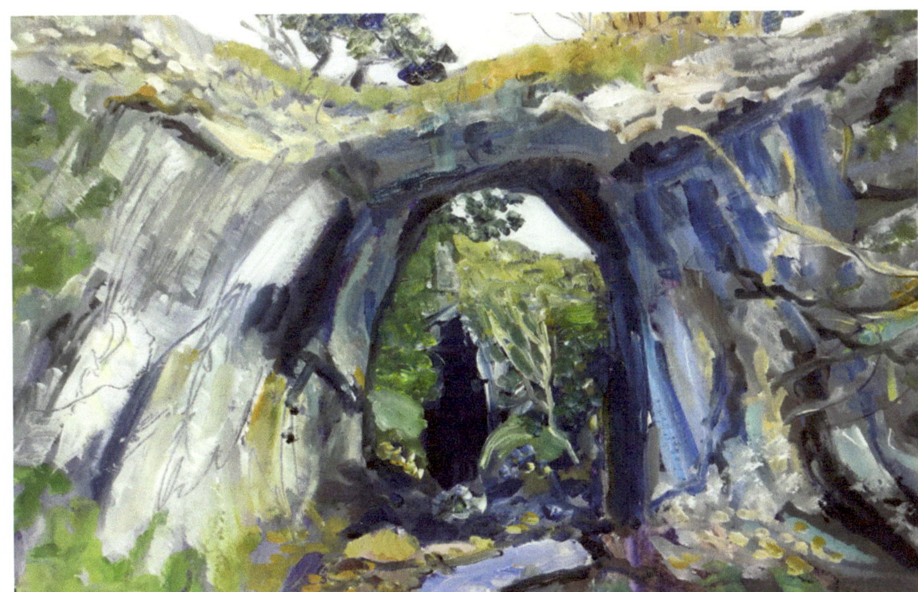

*'Reynards Cave,
Dove Dale'
20th February*

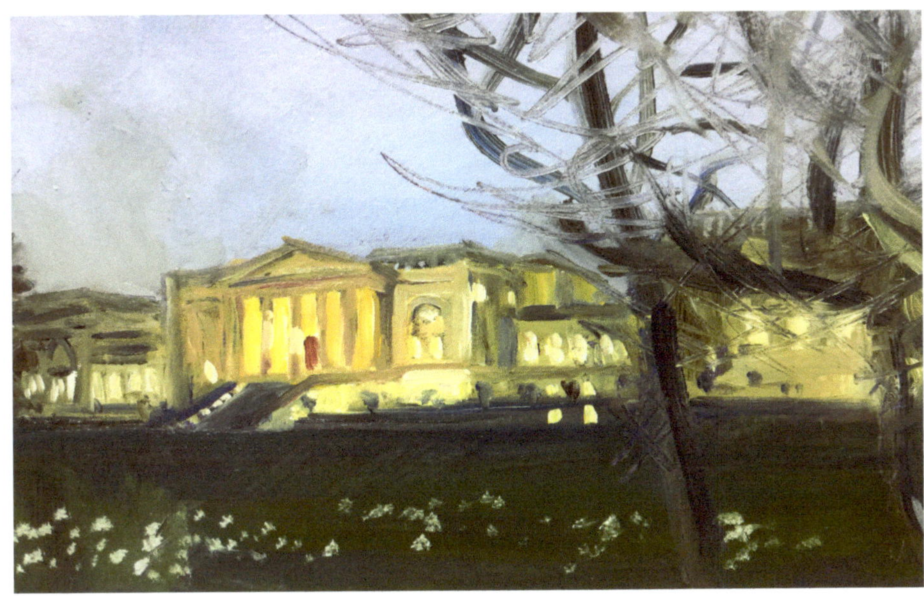

*'Dusk on the South
Front'
28th February*

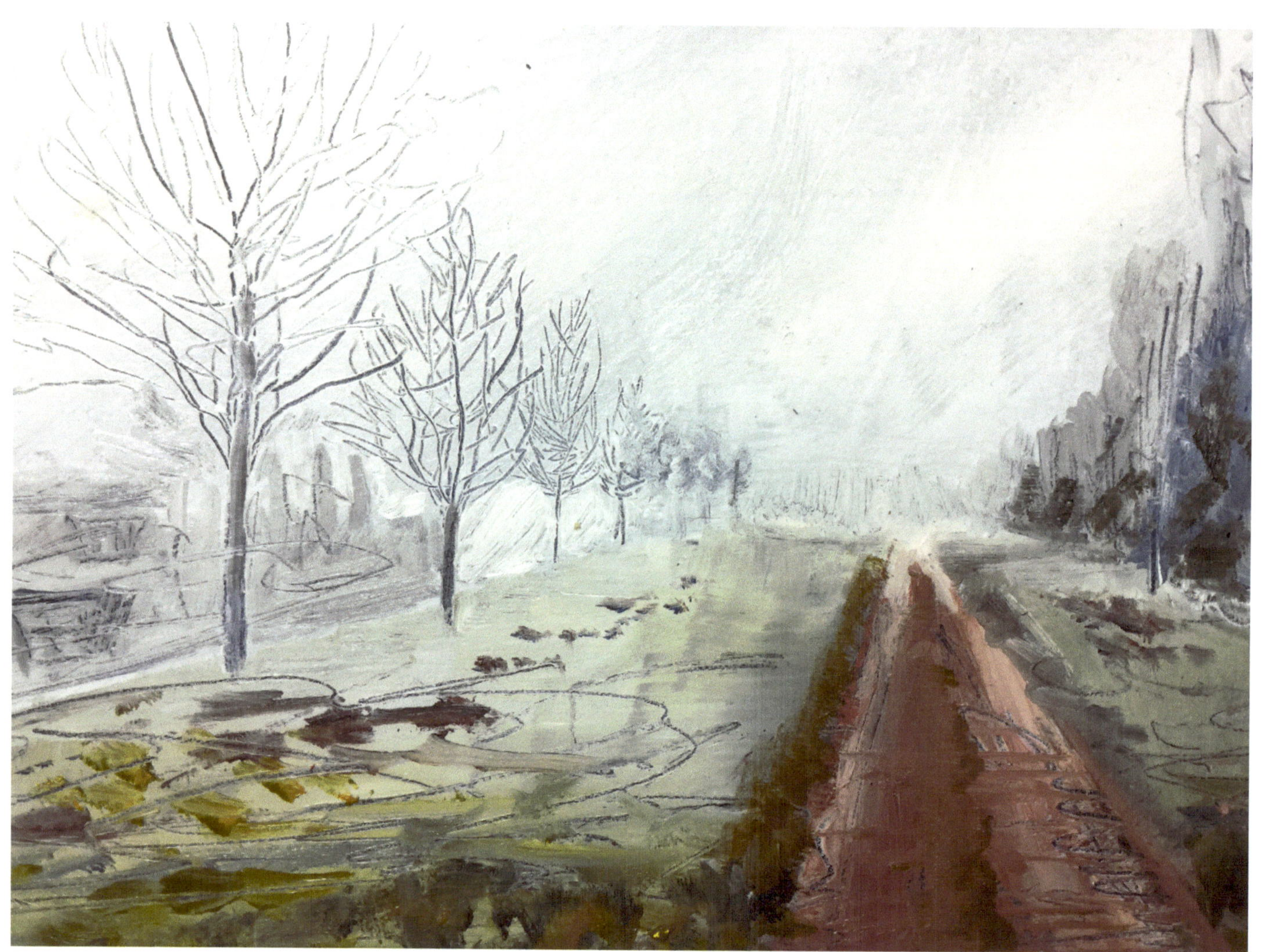

'Fog on the Paddock Course Walk'
10th February

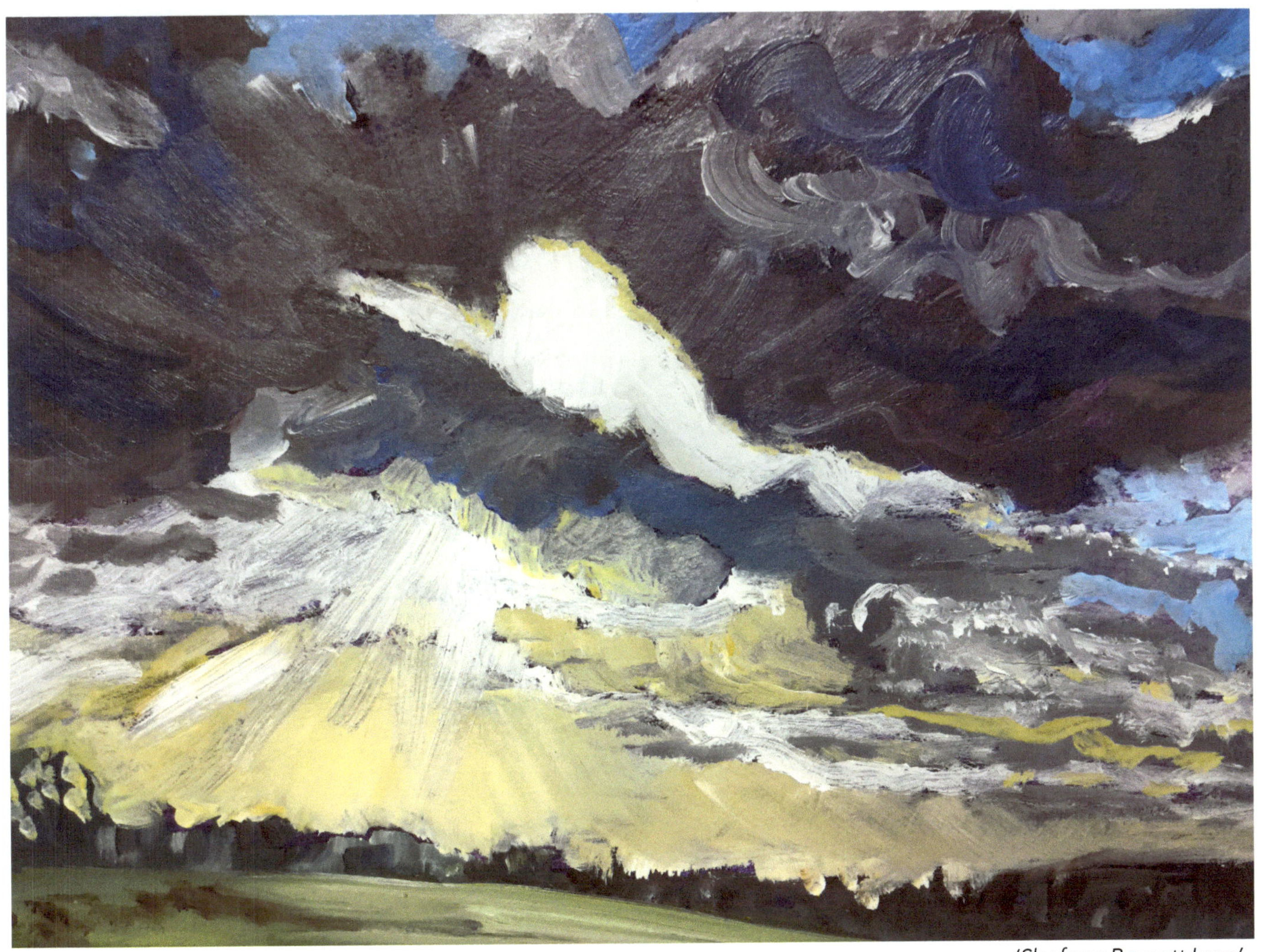

'Sky from Boycott Lane'
24th February

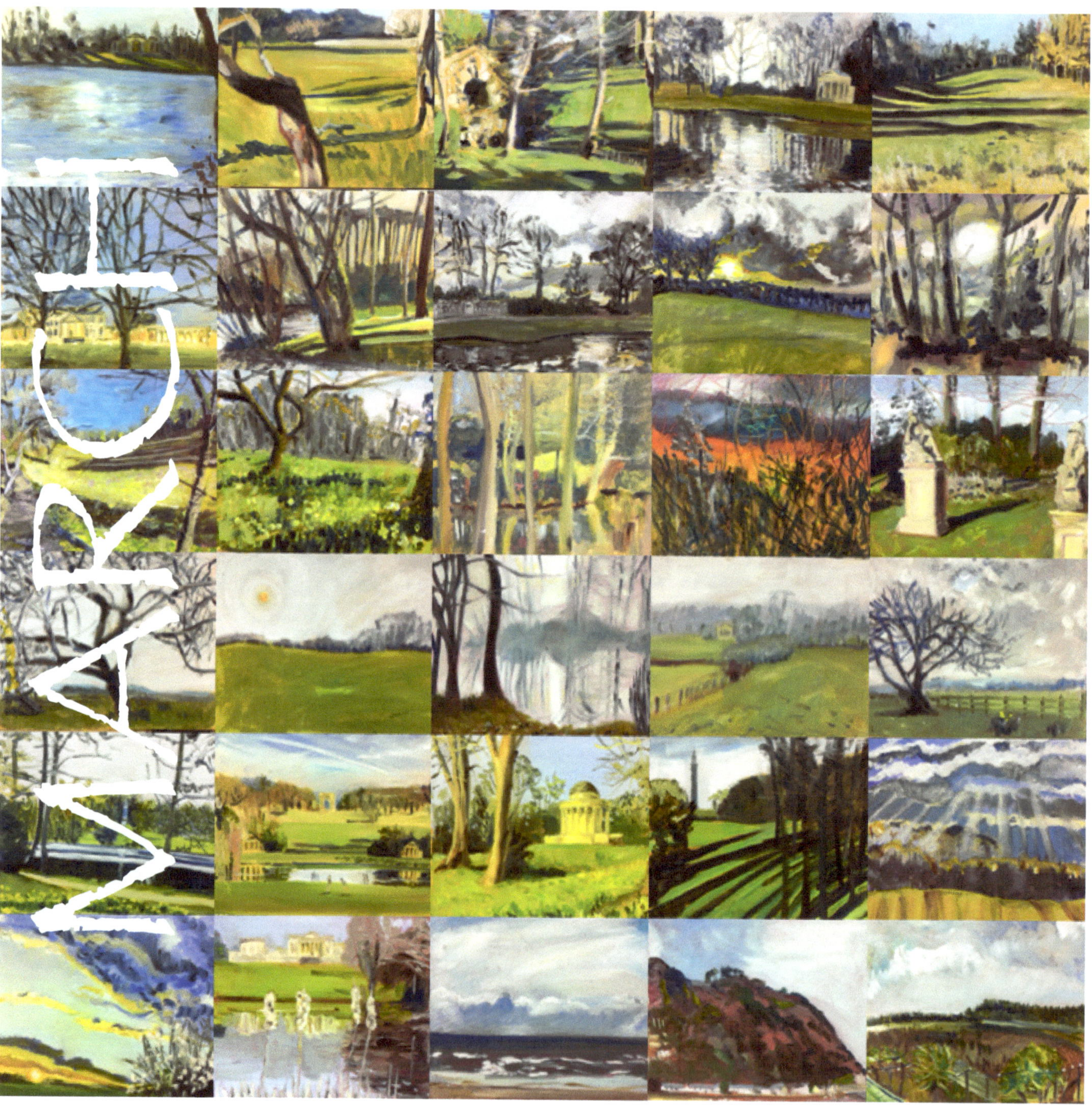
MARCH

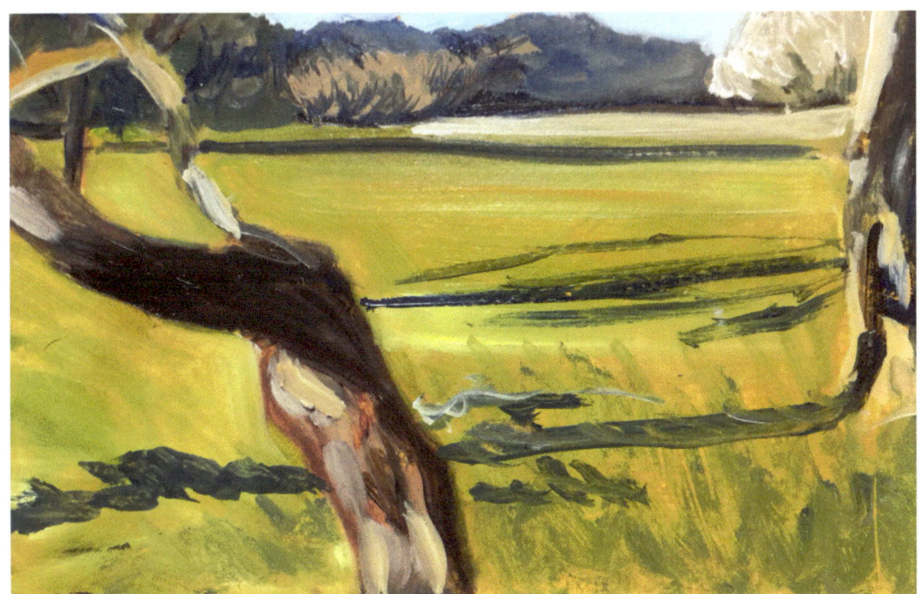

'Trees from the Art School'
2nd March

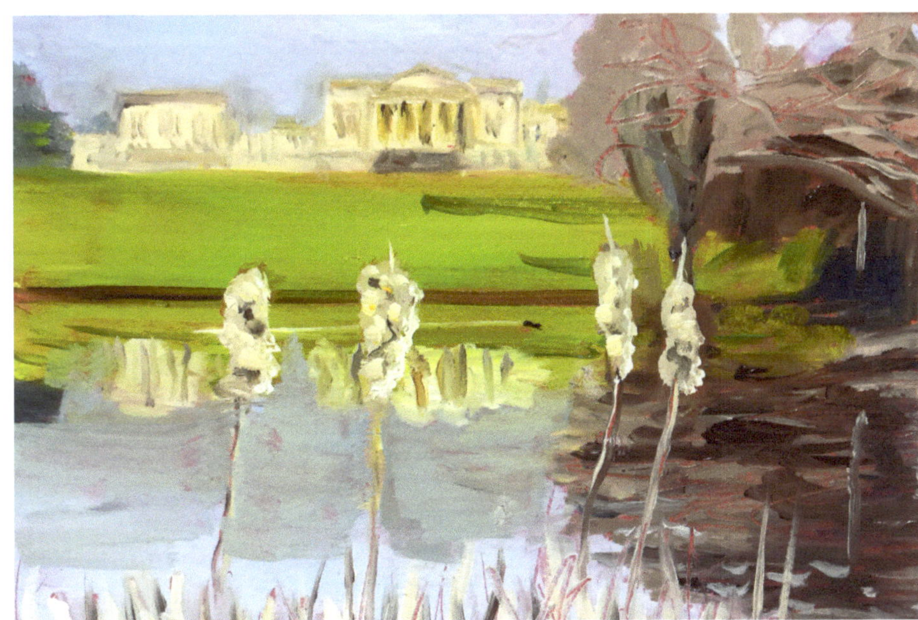

'Bull rushes and the South Front'
27th March

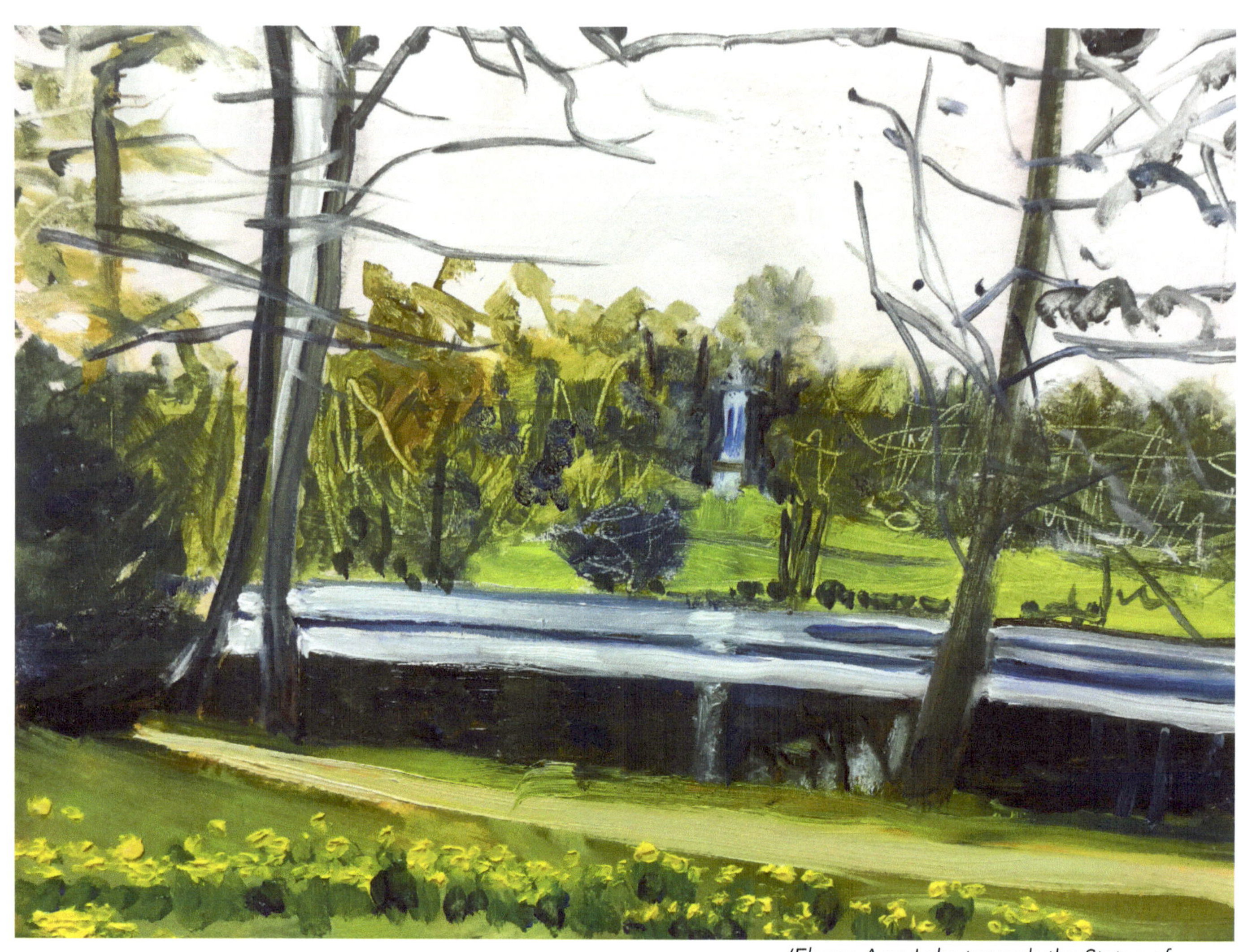

'Eleven Acre Lake towards the Statue of Queen Caroline'
21st March

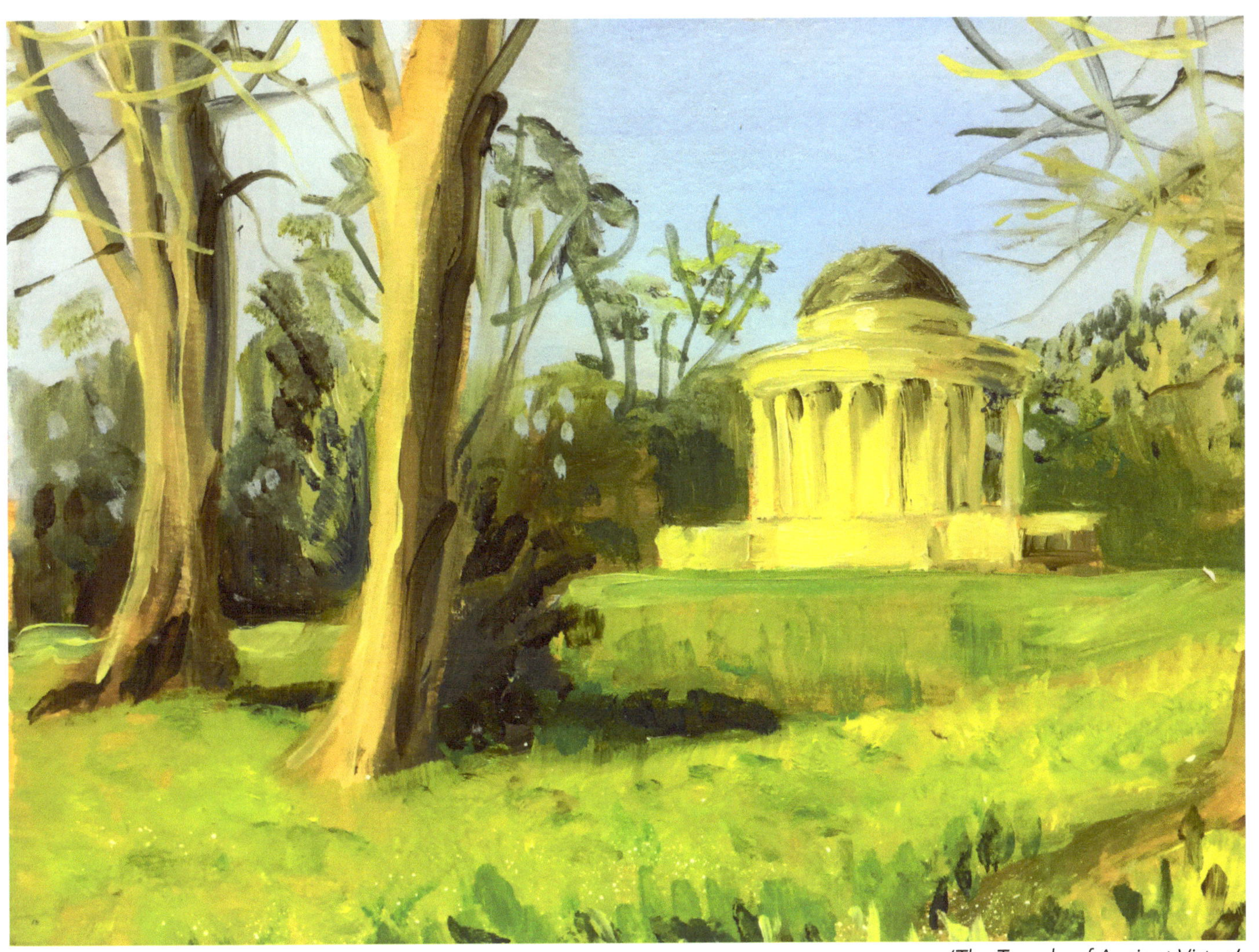

'The Temple of Ancient Virtue'
23rd March

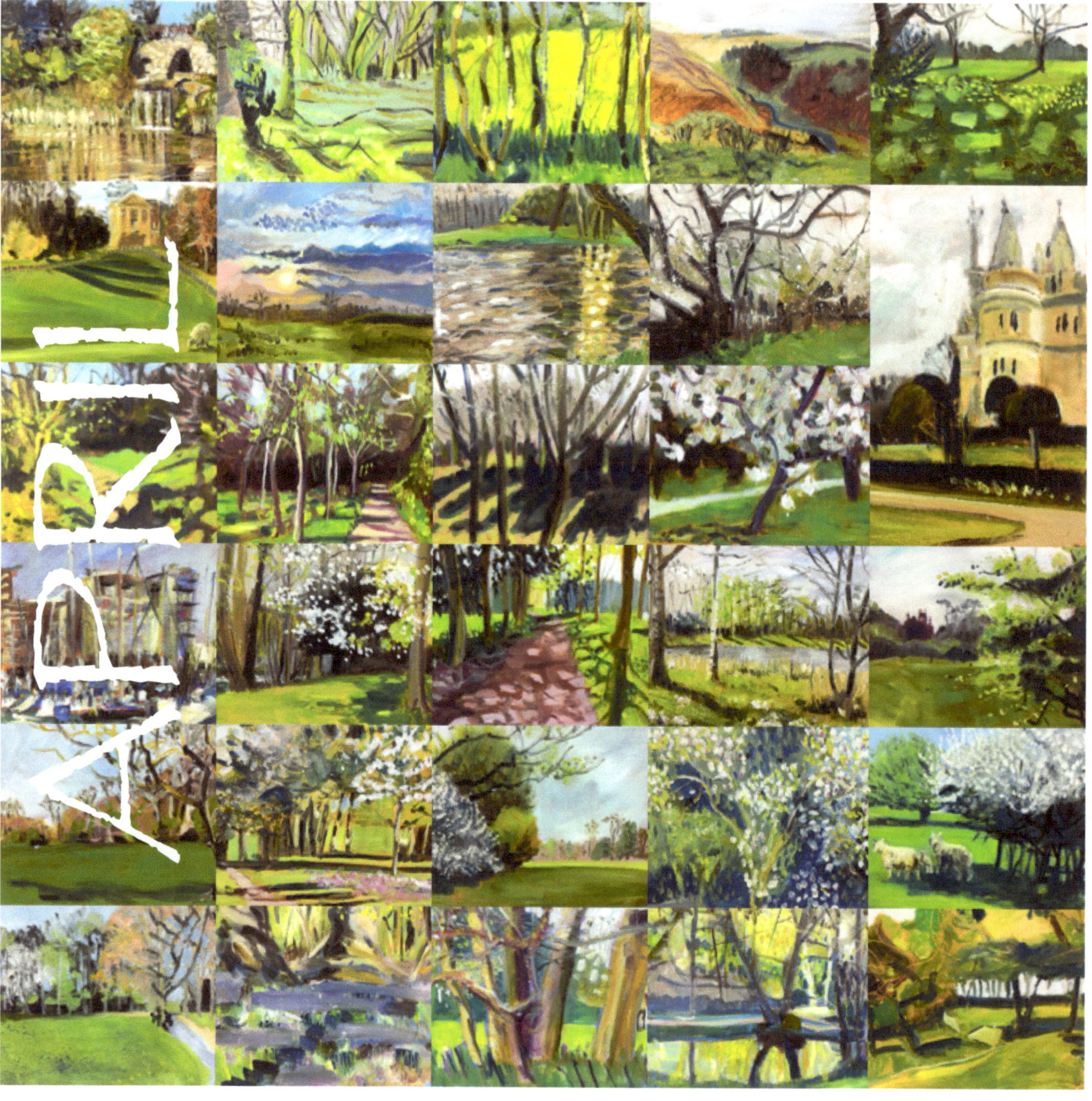
APRIL

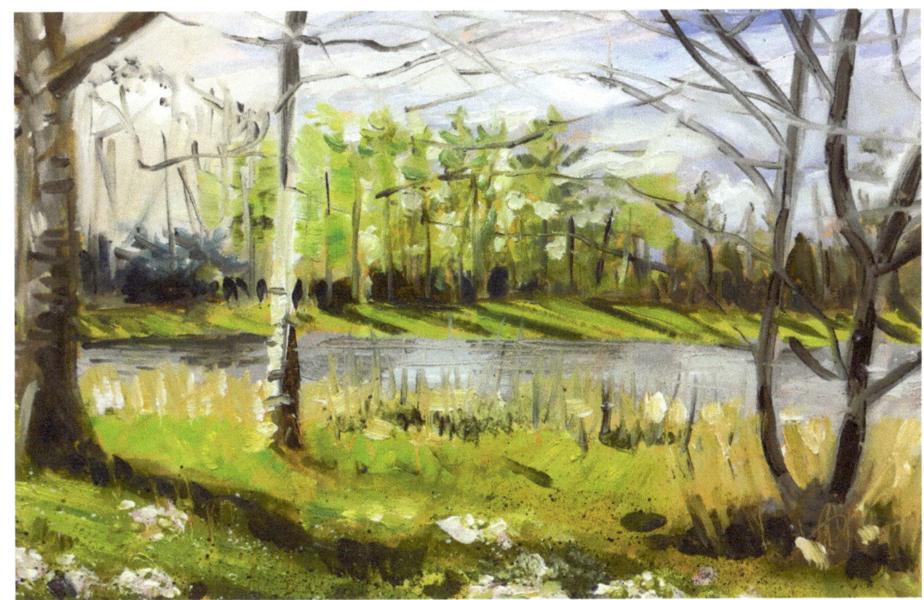

'Across the Octagon Lake'
17th April

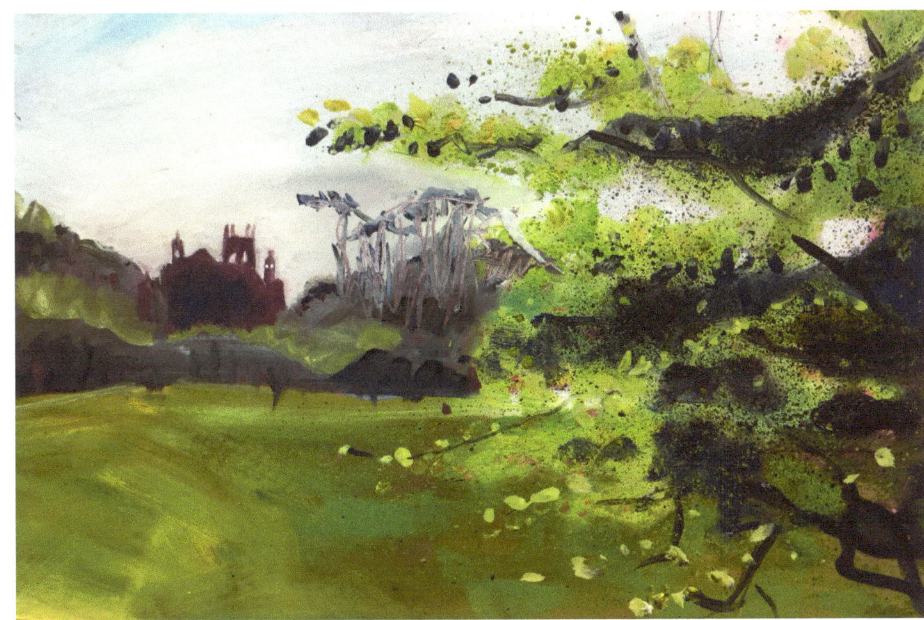

'From Stowe Castle to the Gothic Temple'
20th April

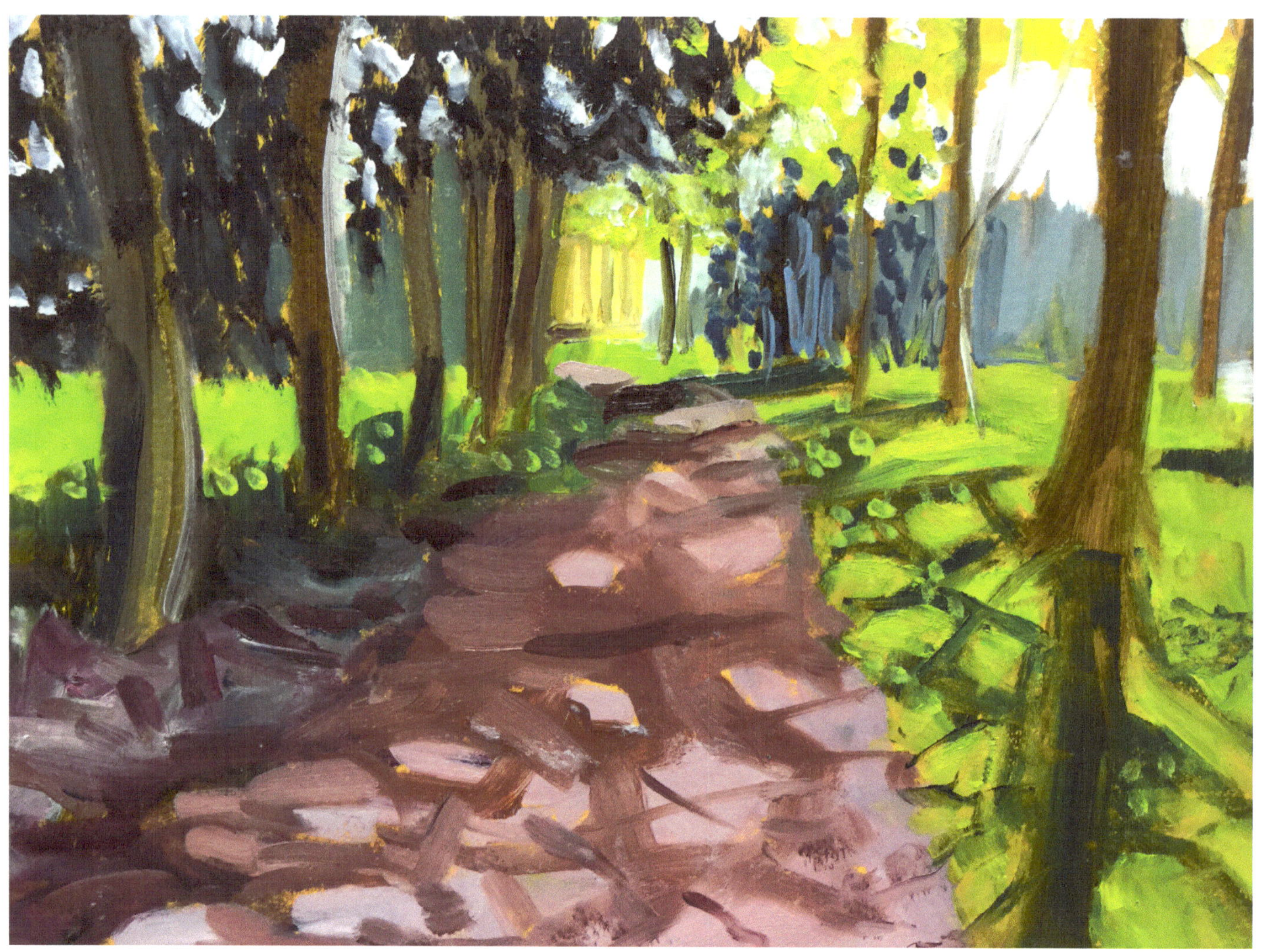

'Towards the Eastern Lake Pavilion'
19th April

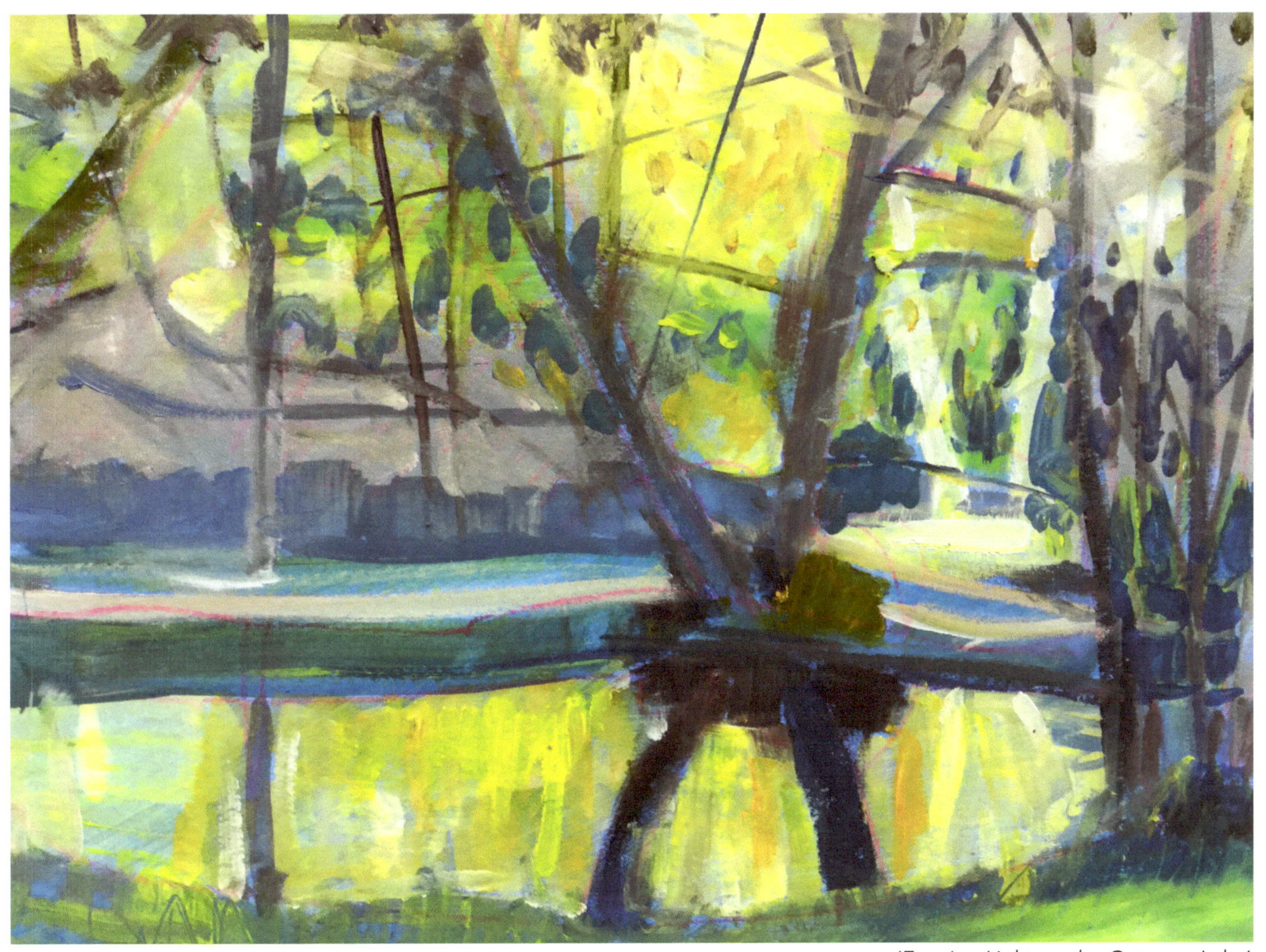

'Evening Light on the Octagon Lake'
30th April

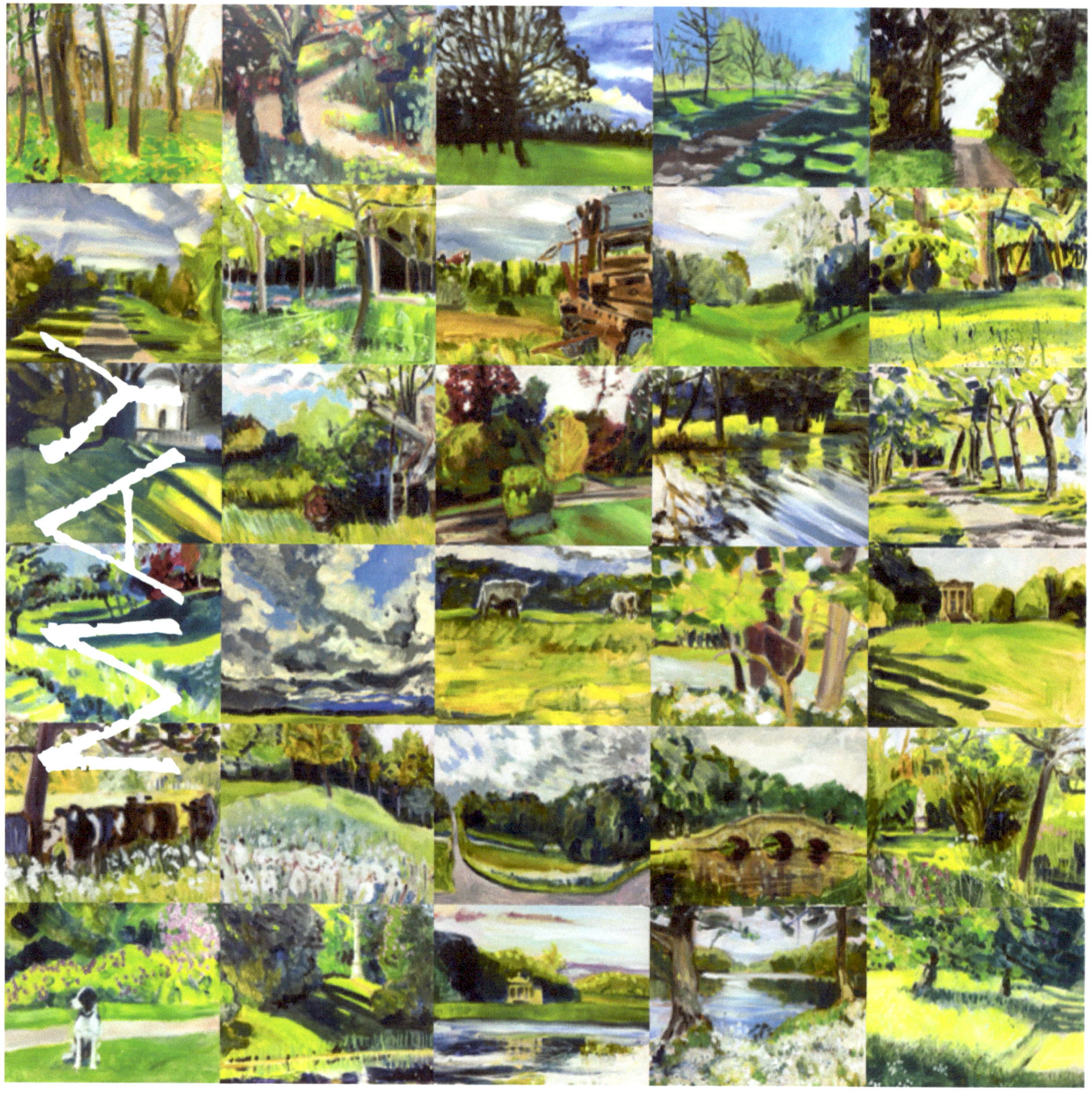
MAY

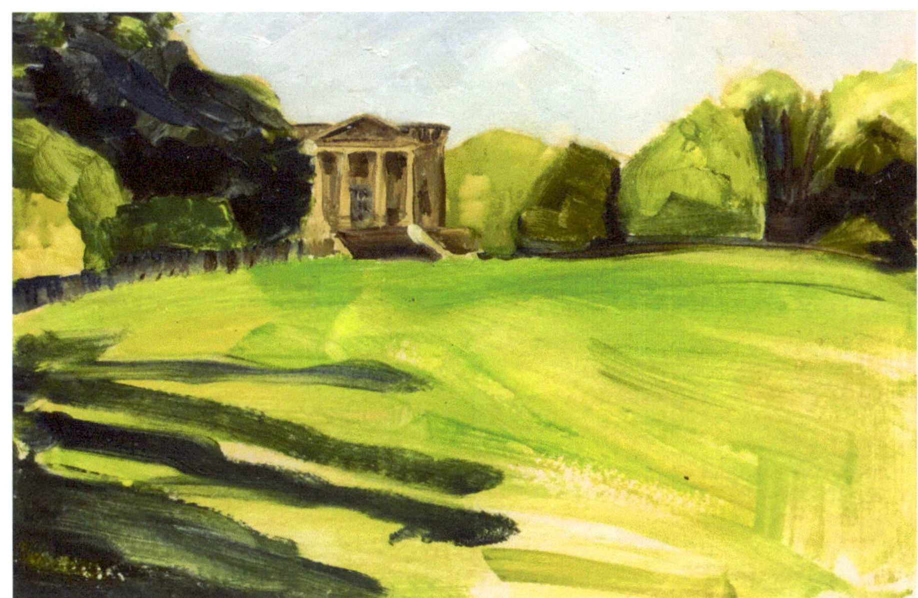

'The Queen's Temple'
21st May

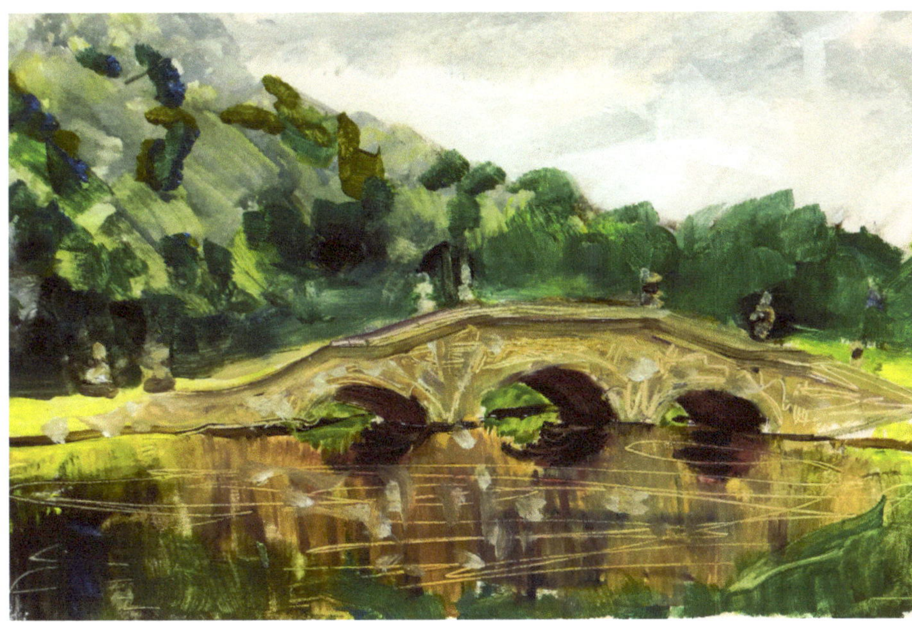

'The Oxford Bridge'
25th May

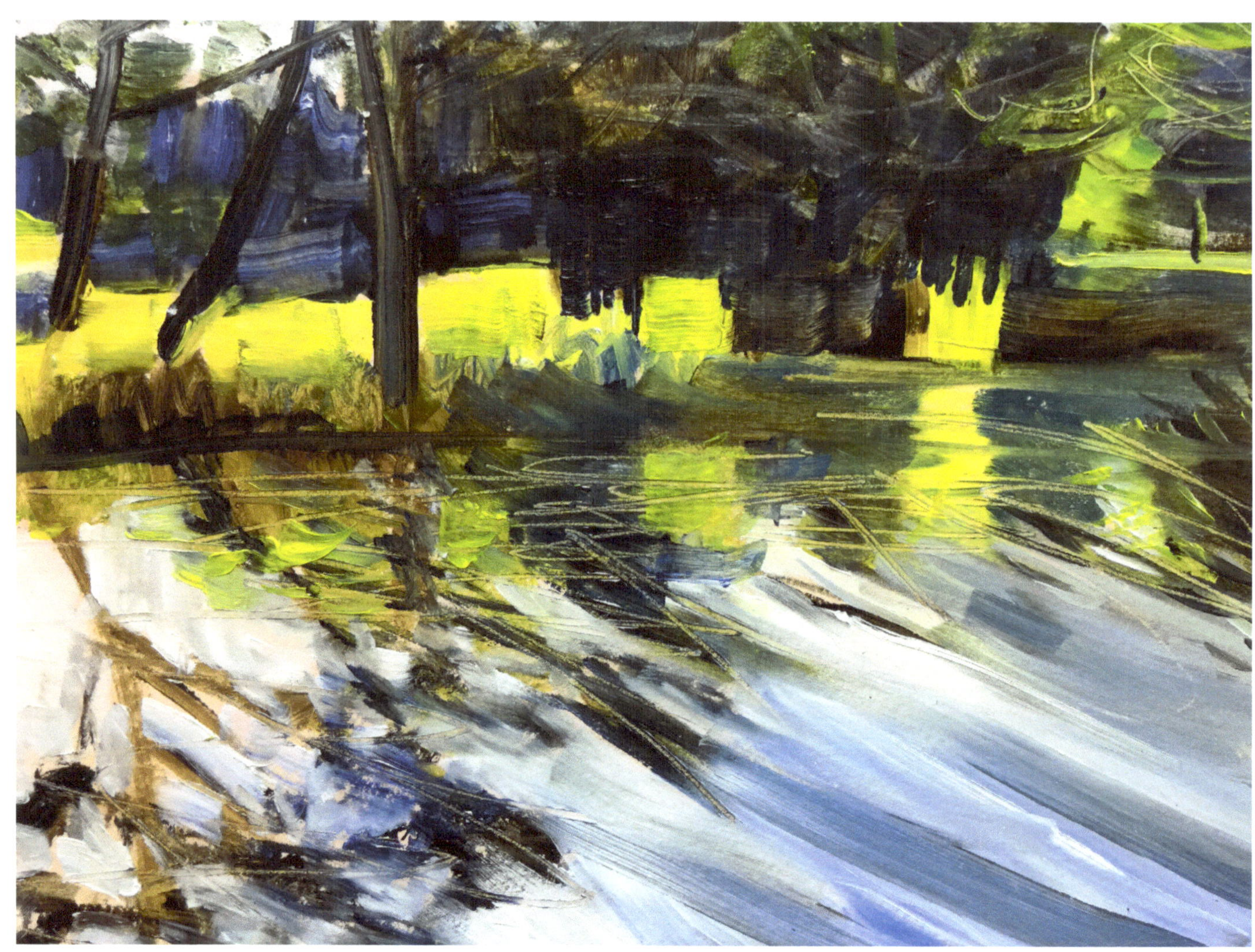

'Reflections on the Octagon Lake'
15th May

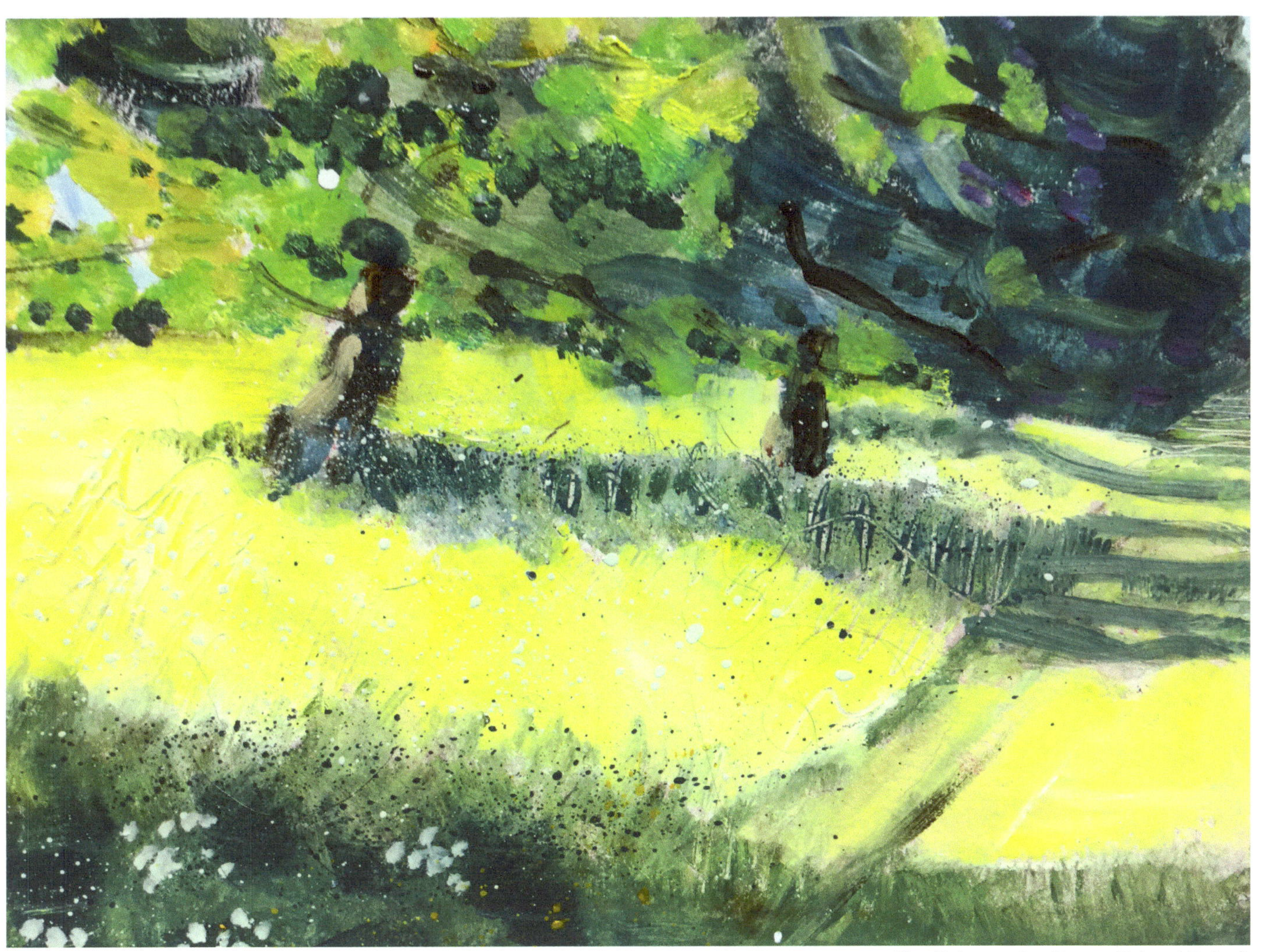

'Sunlight on the Stowe School Drive'
31st May

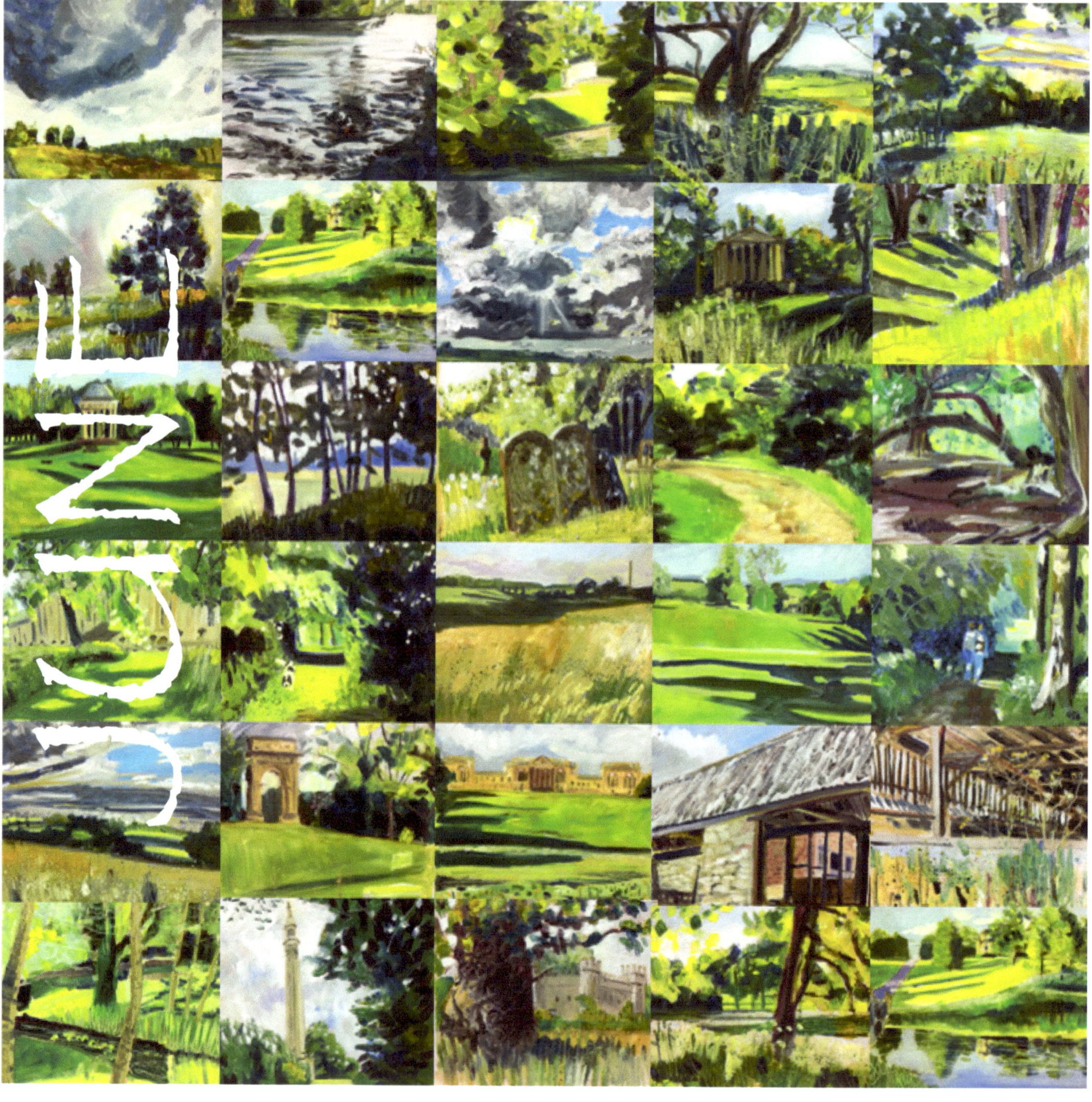
JUNE

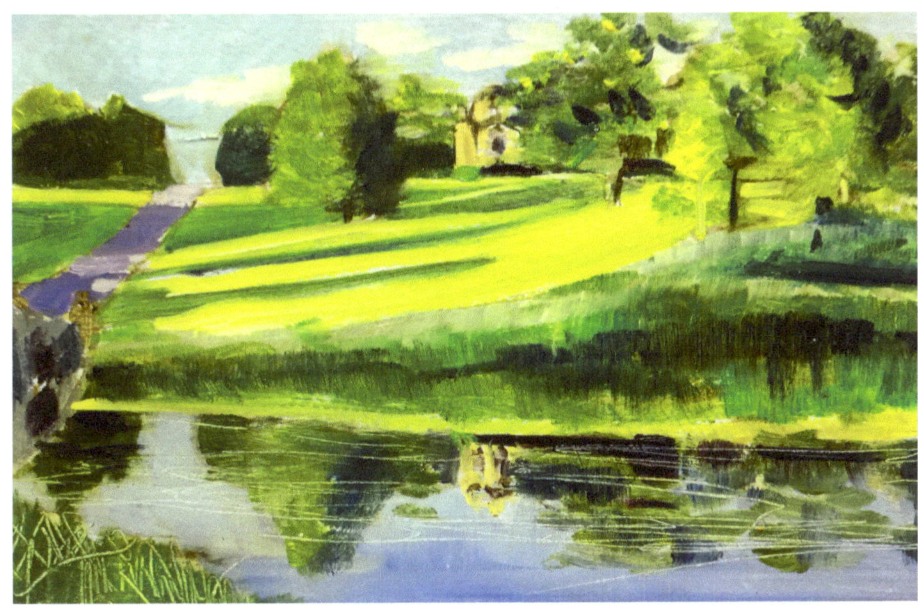

'Across the Oxford Water to the Boycott Pavillions' 7th June

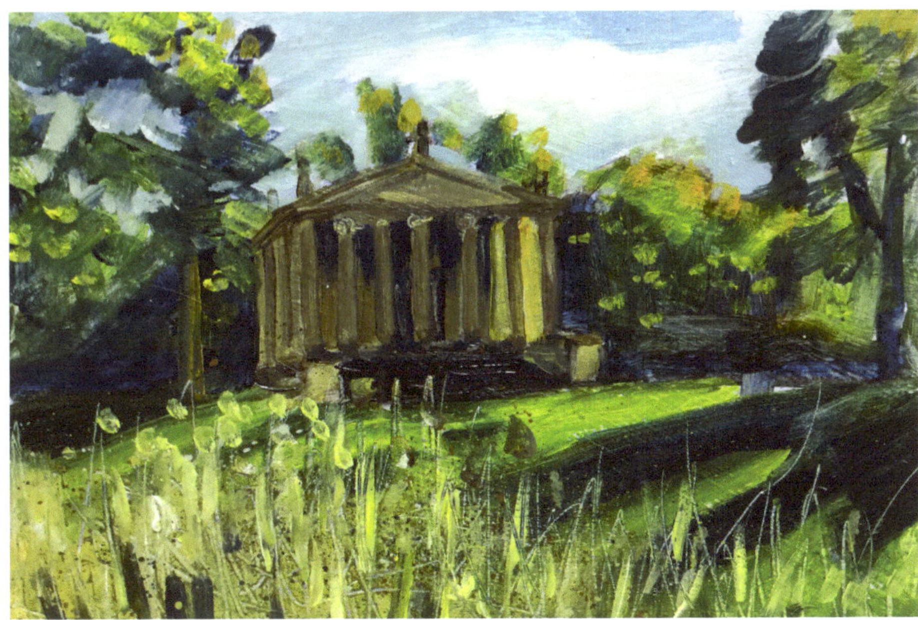

'The Temple of Concord and Victory' 9th June

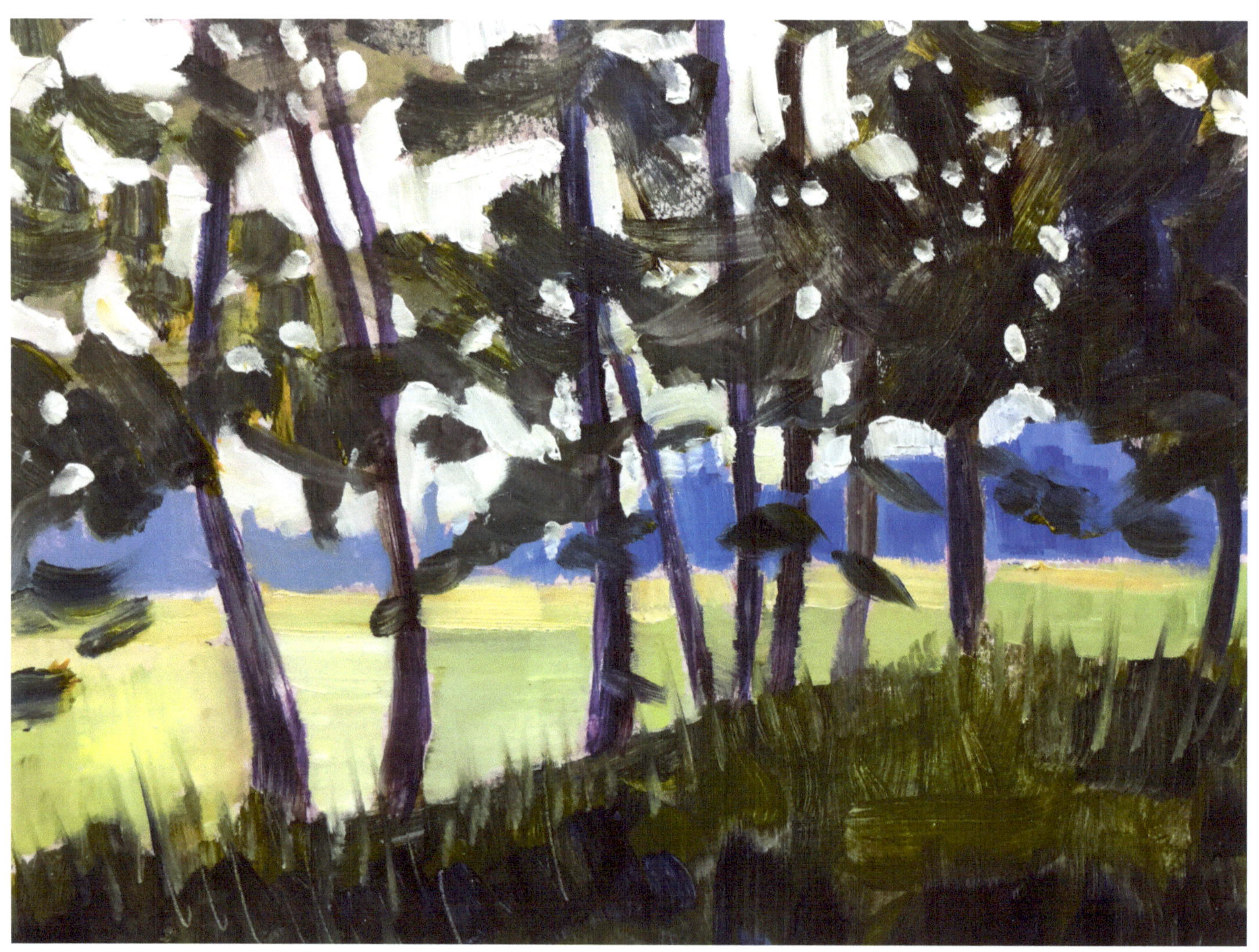

'Rainy Day Light'
12th June

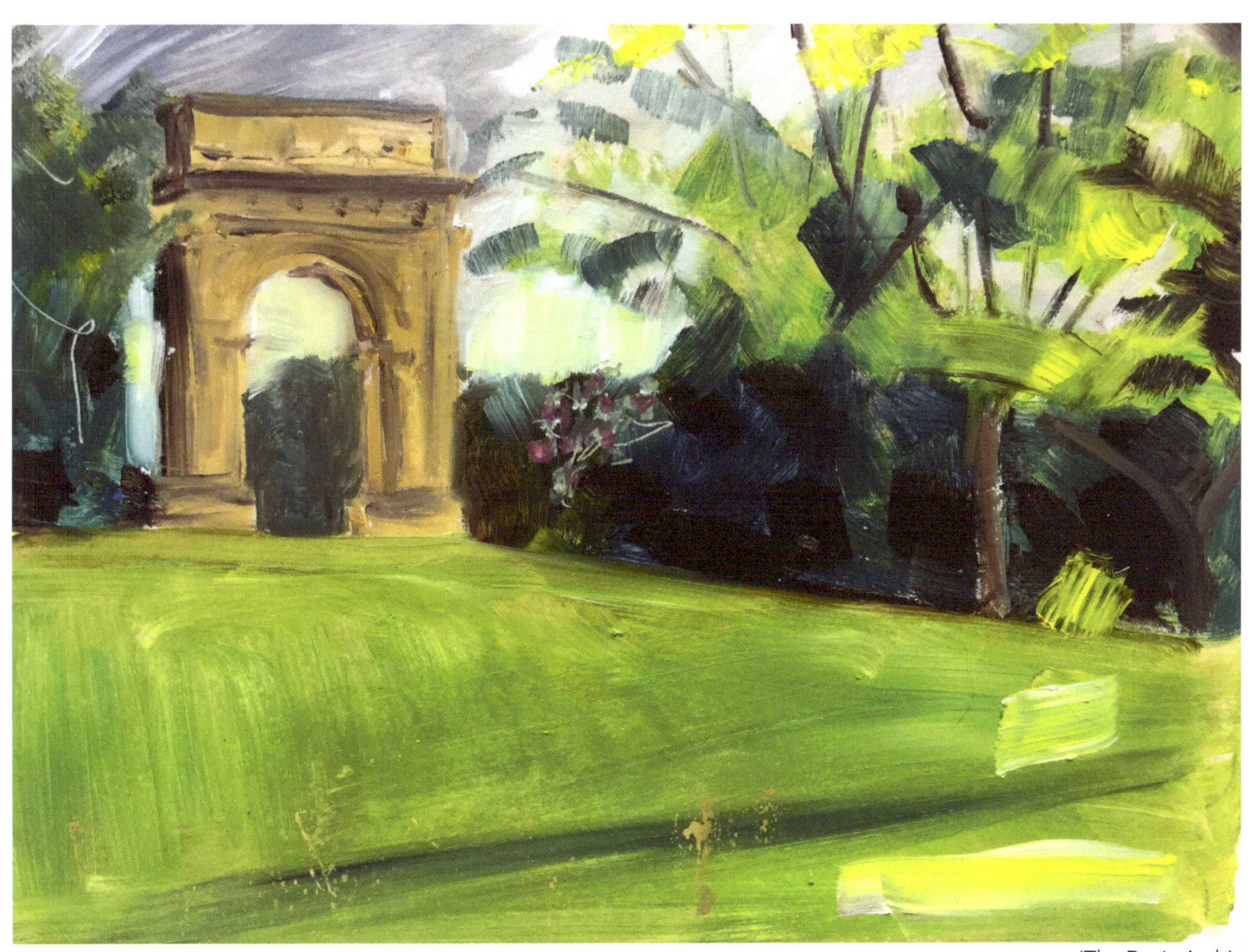

'The Doric Arch'
22nd June

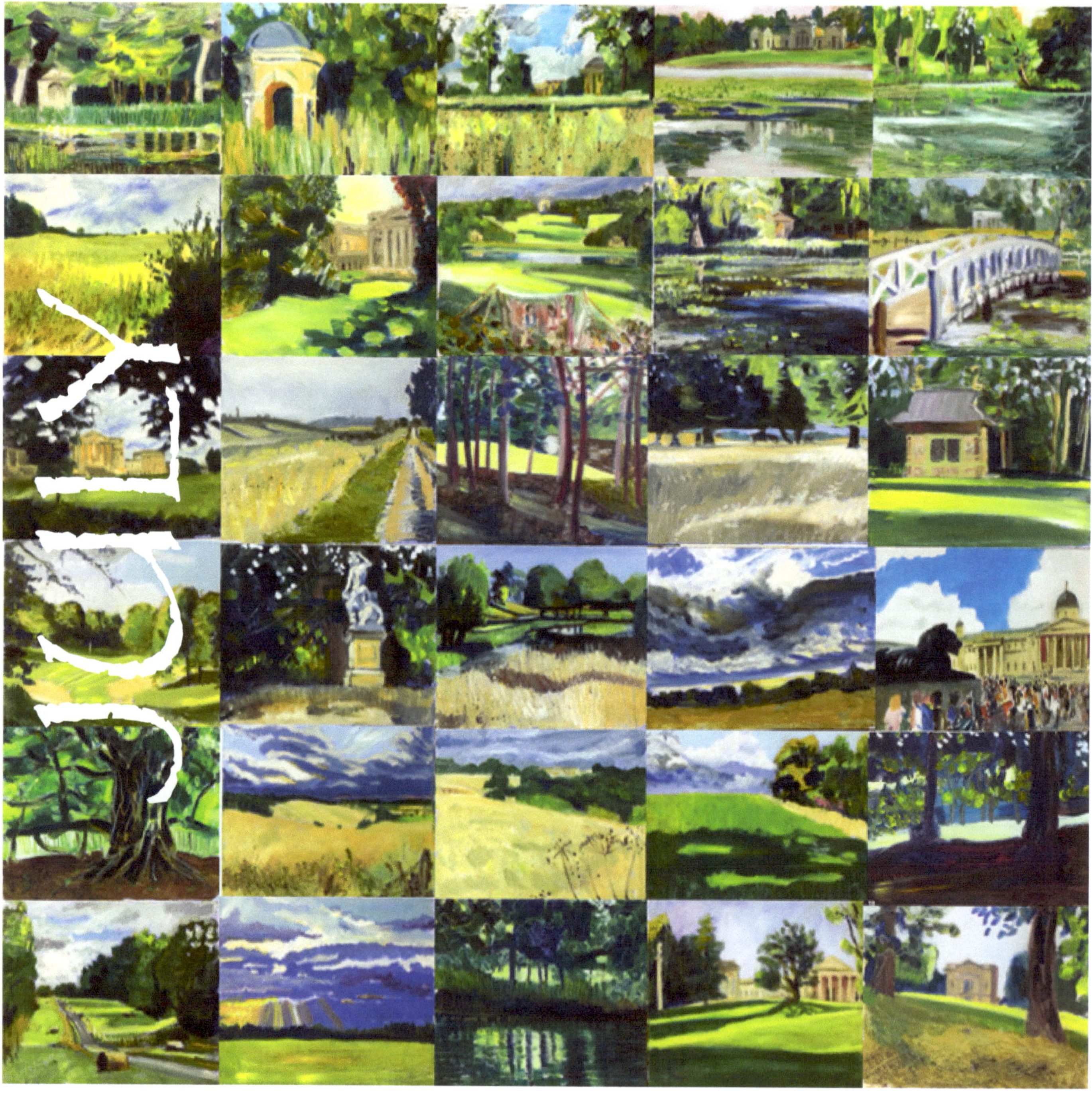
July

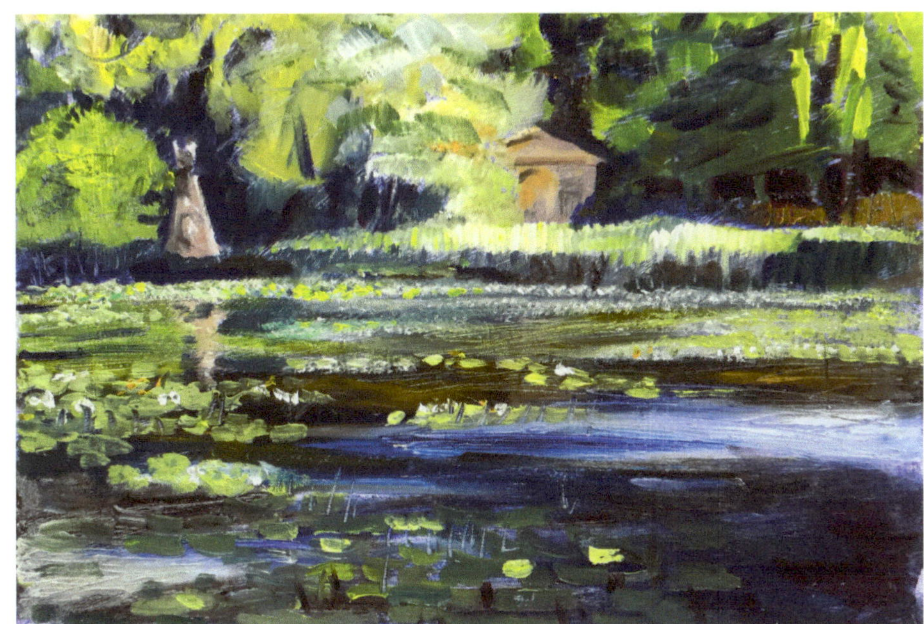

'Monkey Island from the Octagon Lake'
10th July

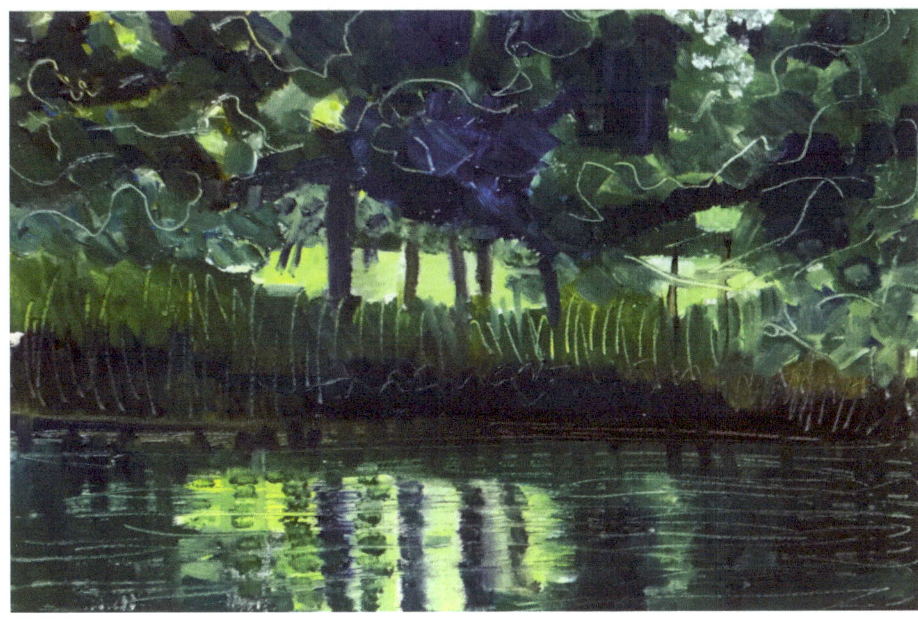

'Tree Spaces reflecting on the lake'
29th July

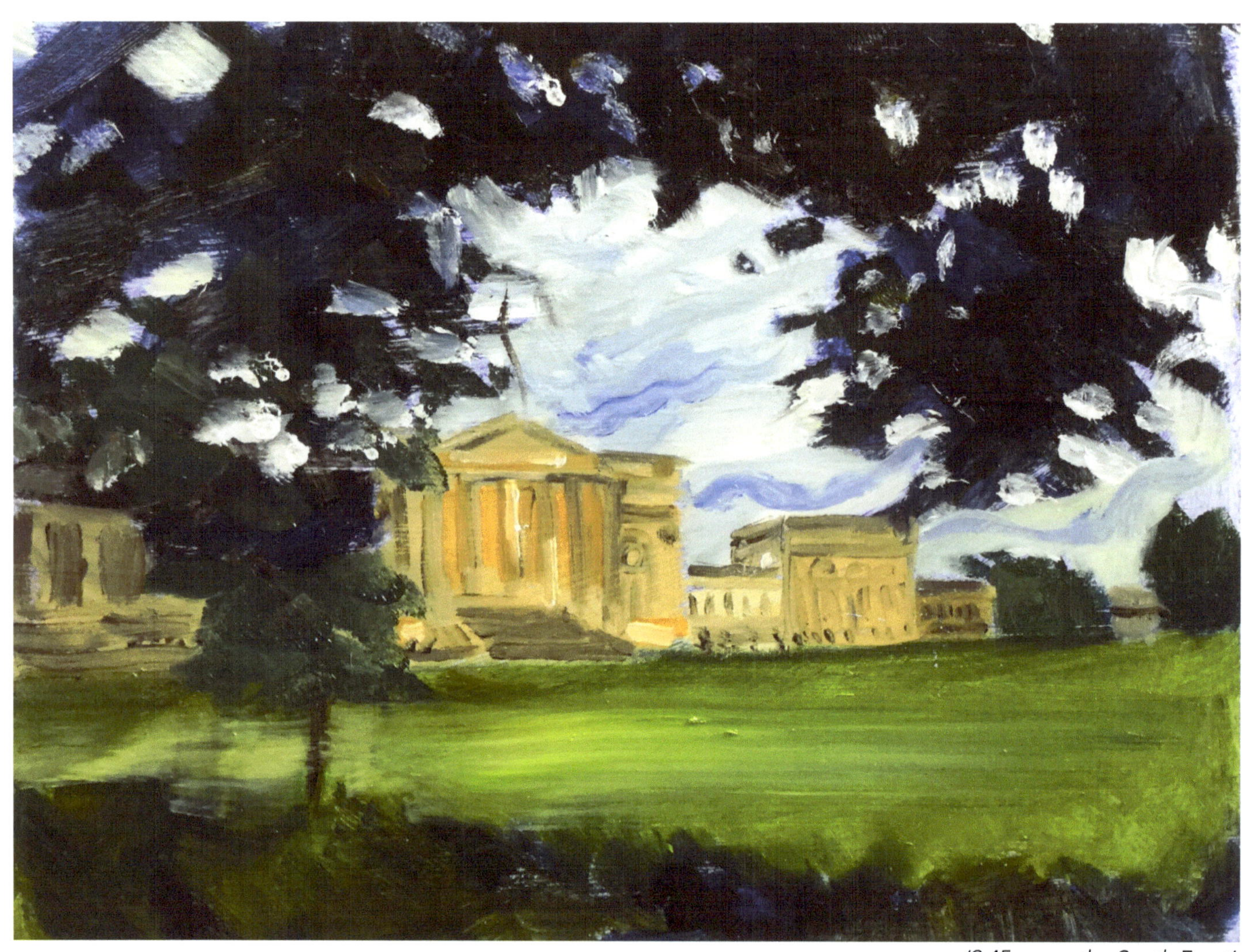

'9:45pm on the South Front'
12th July

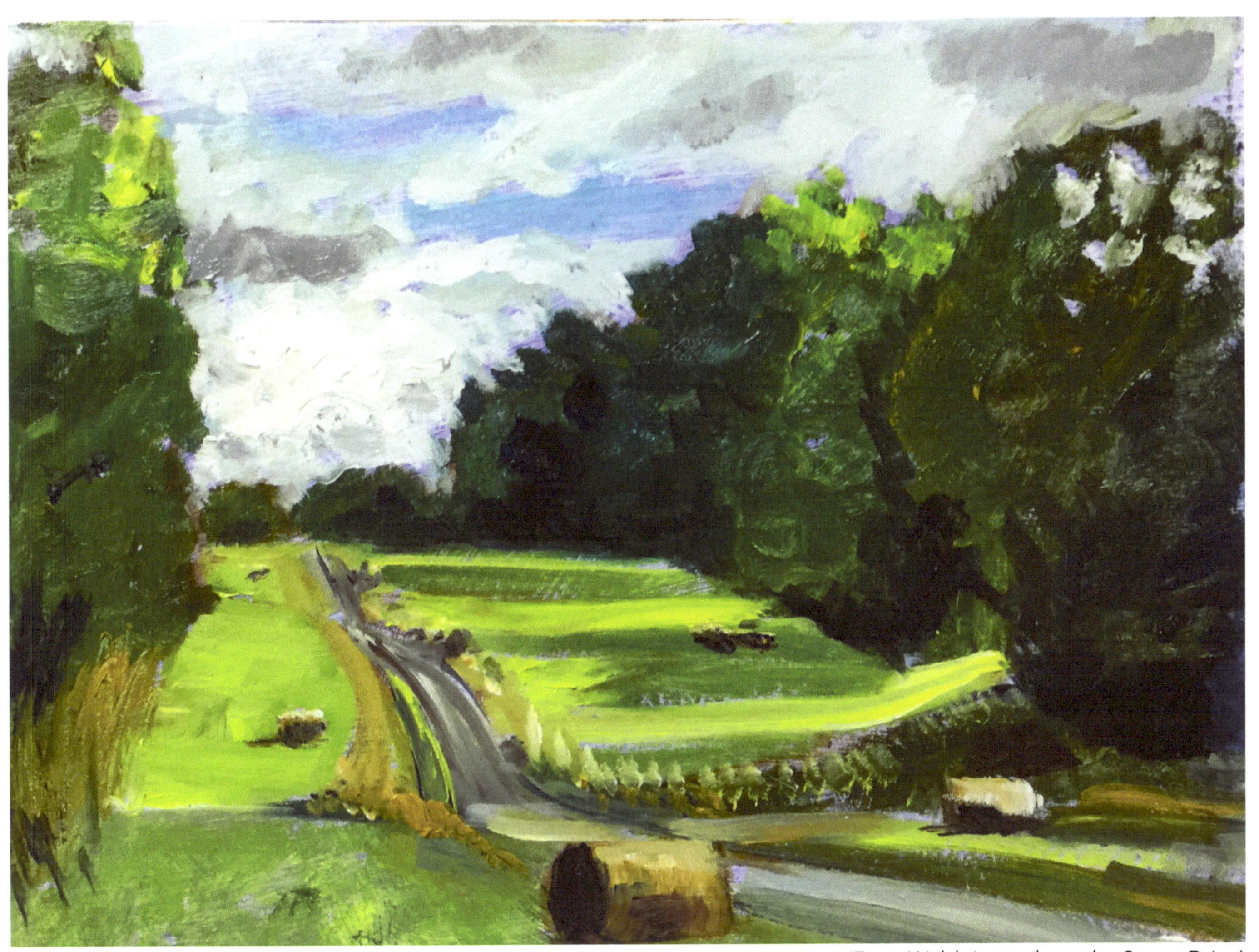

'From Welsh Lane along the Stowe Drive'
27th July

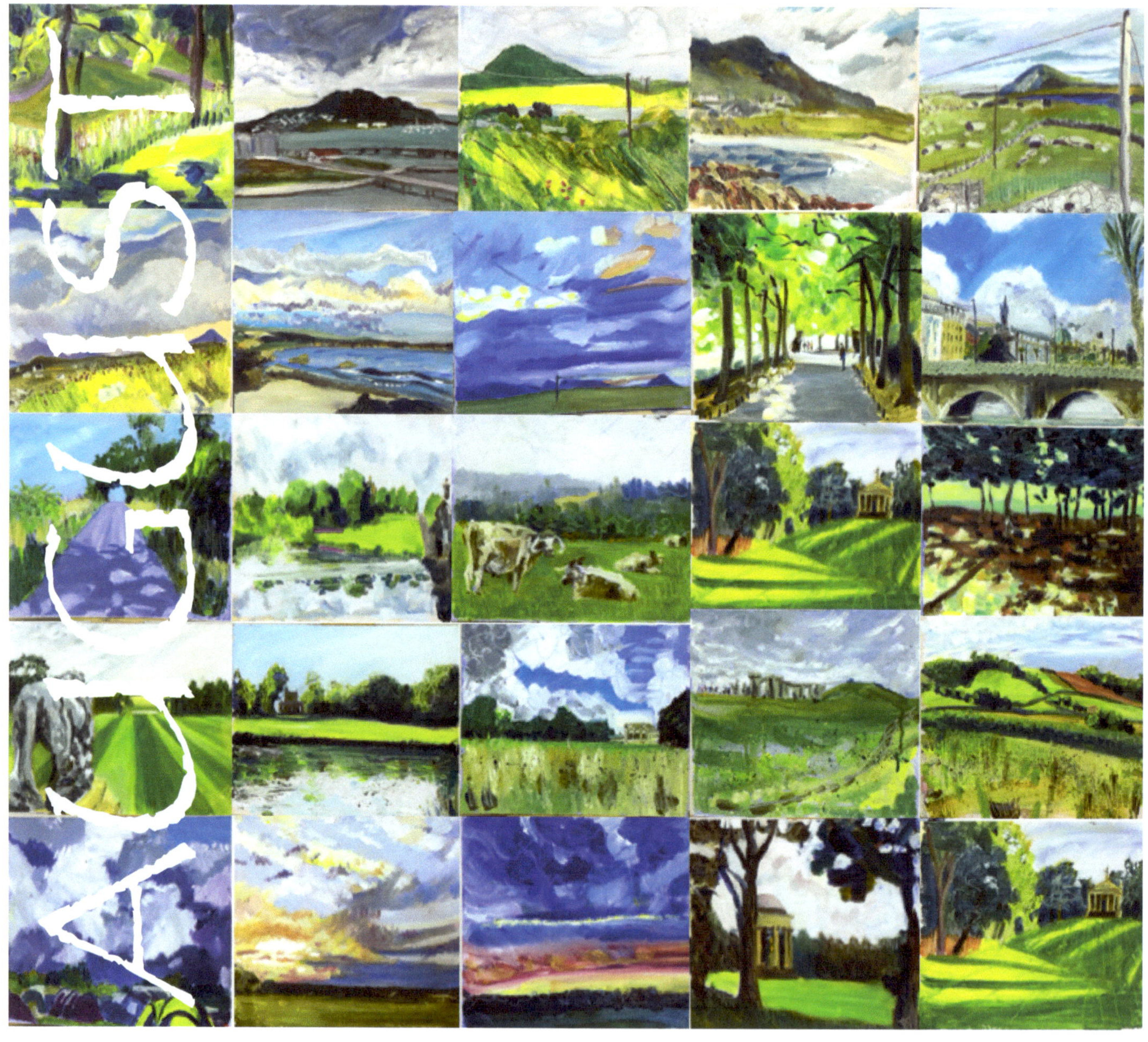
AGIST

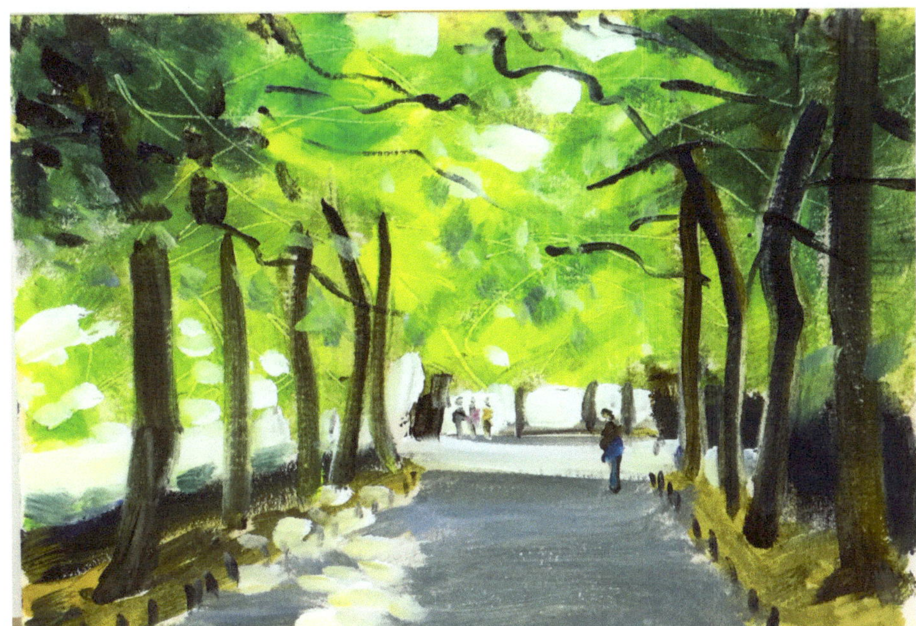

'Lime Walk, St Stephen's Green, Dublin'
9th August

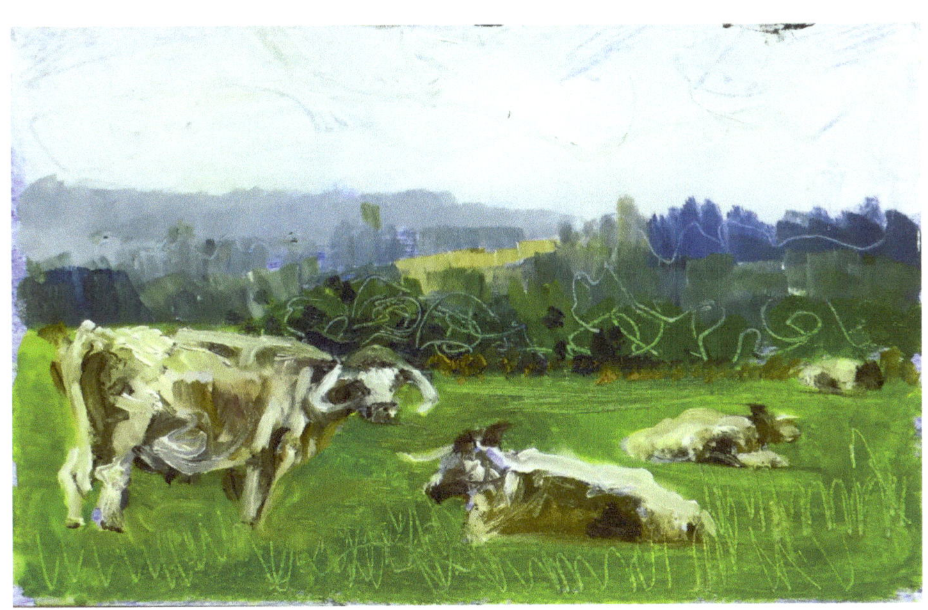

'Rare Cows on the Stowe Drive'
14th August

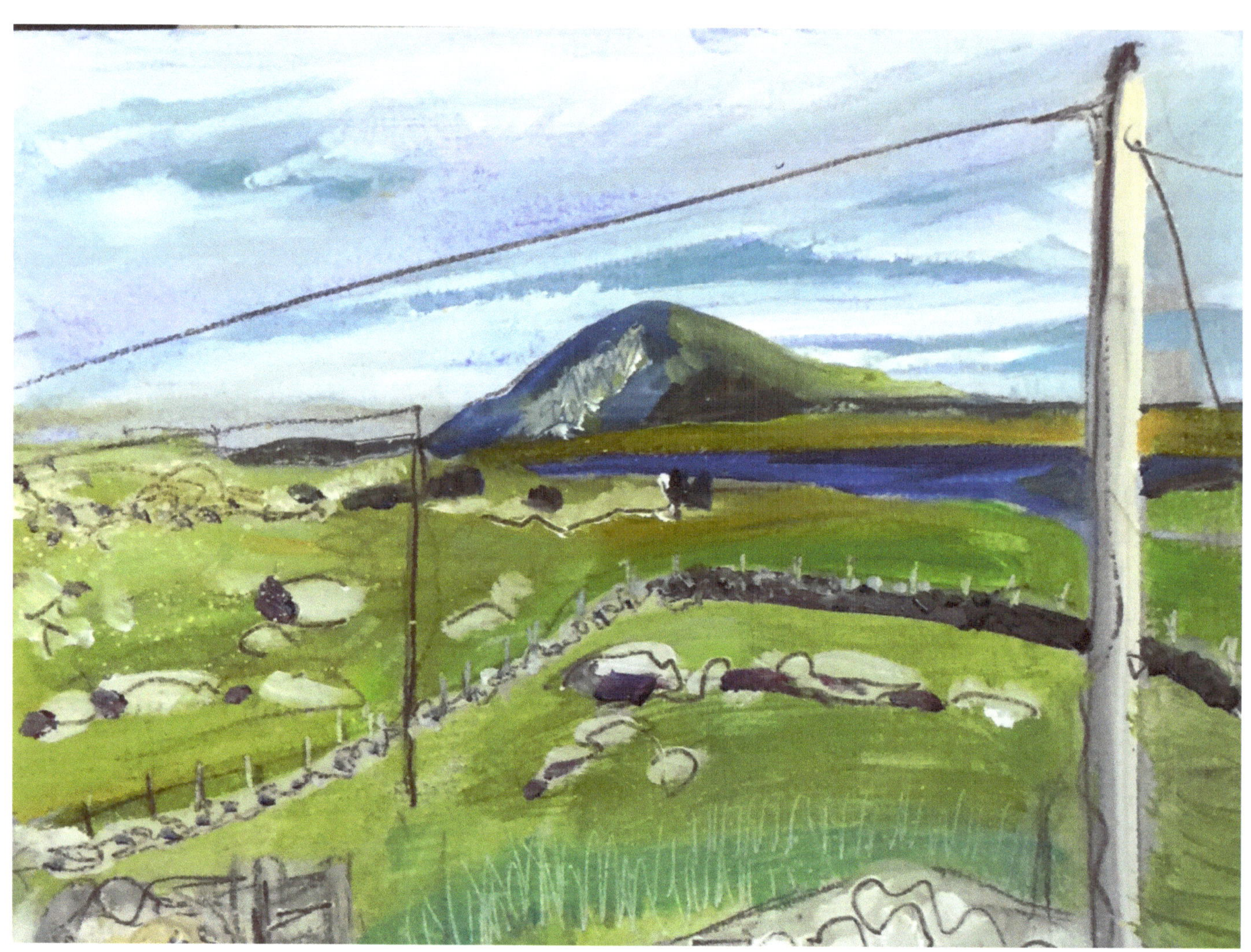

'View from the Pink House, Ireland'
5th August

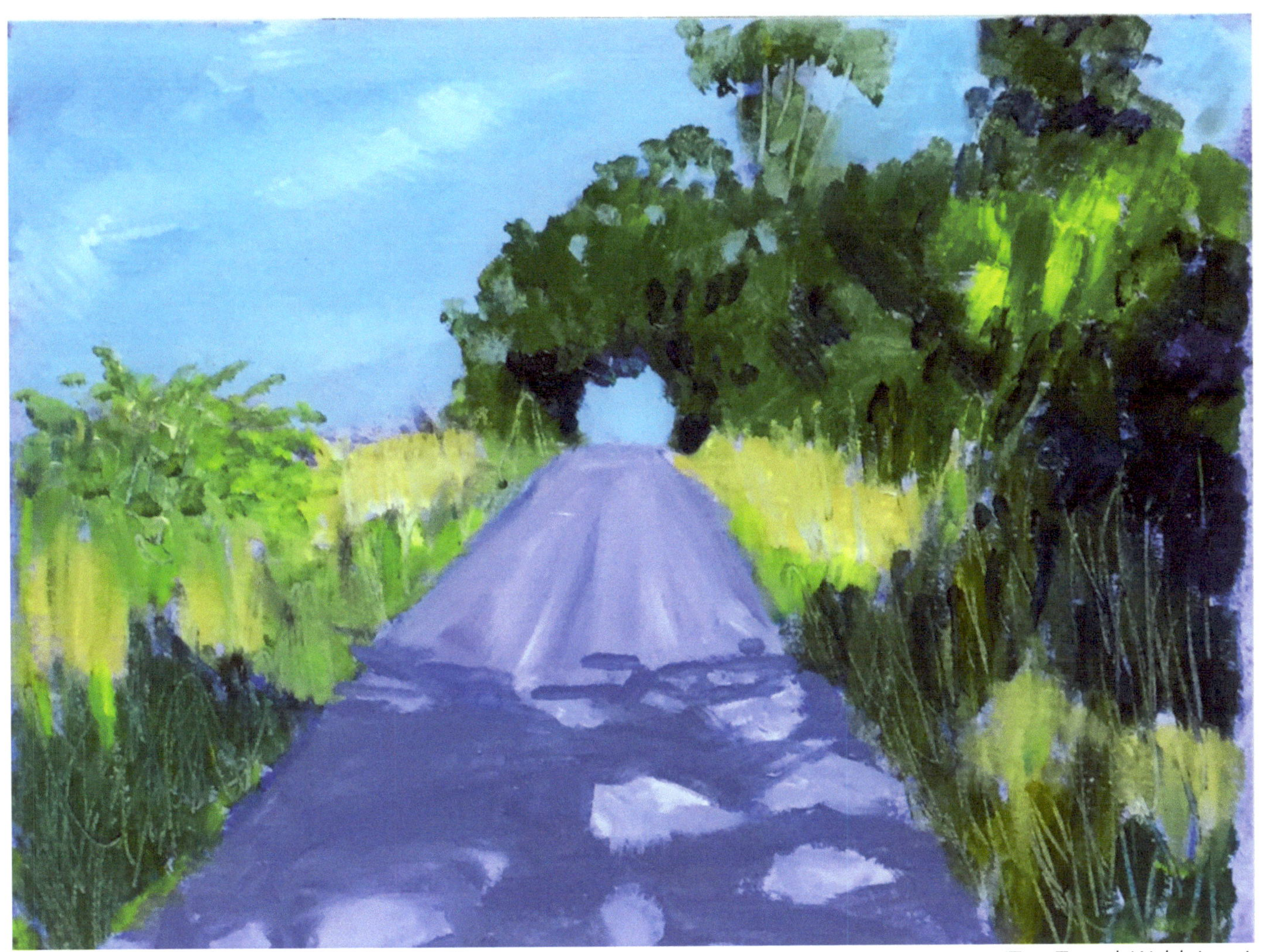

'Tree Tunnel, Welsh Lane'
12th August

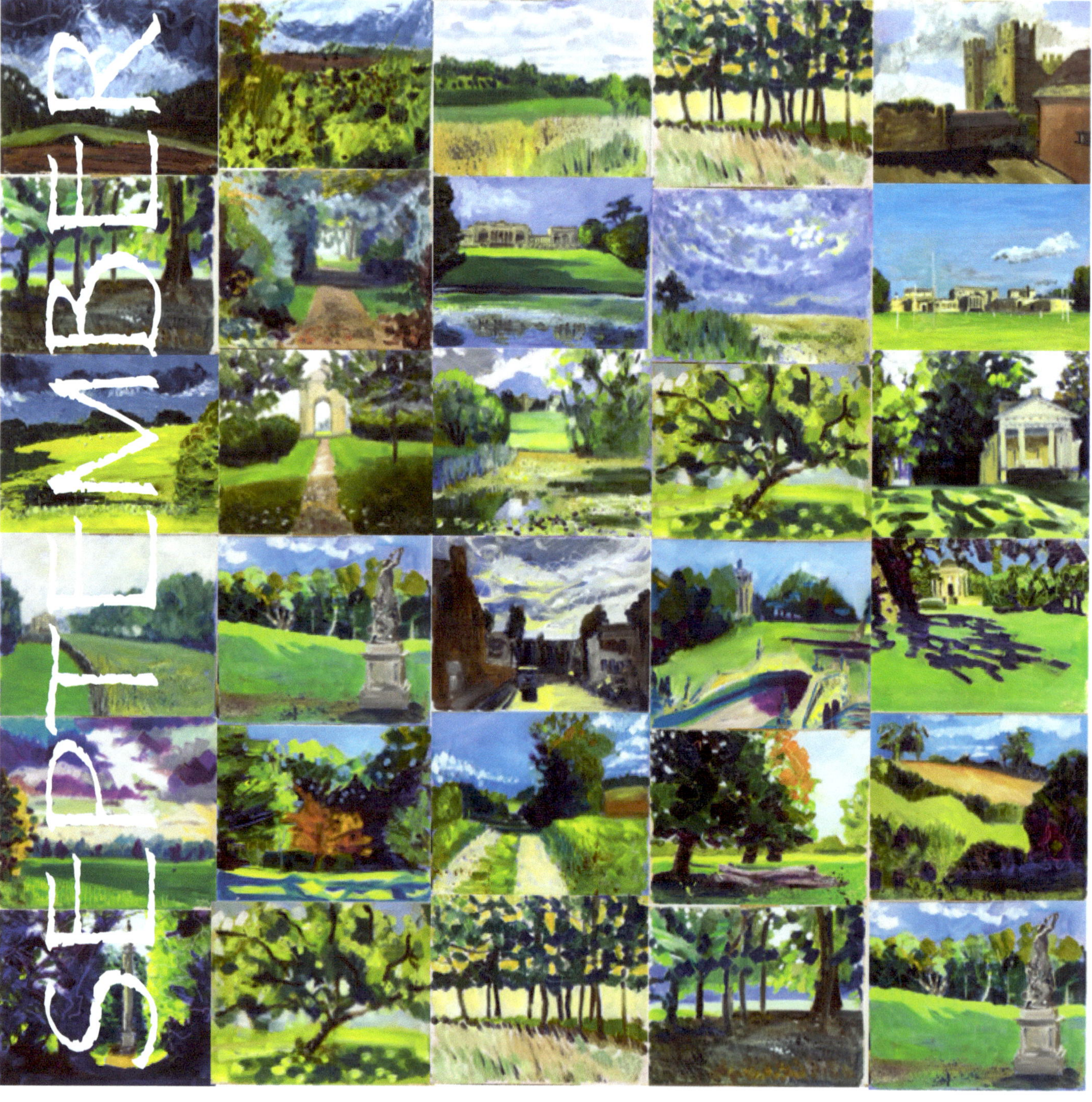
SEPTEMBER

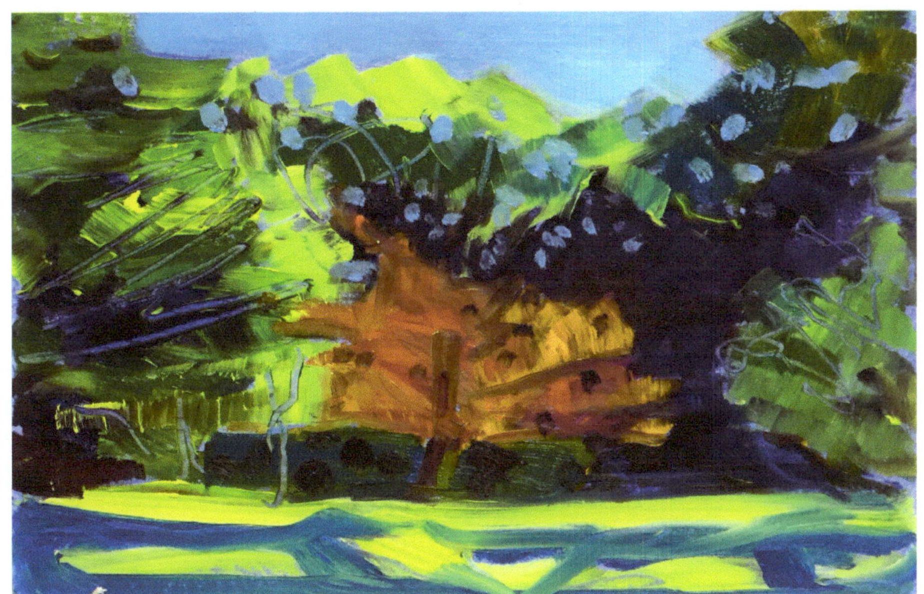

'The Harbinger of Autumn'
26th September

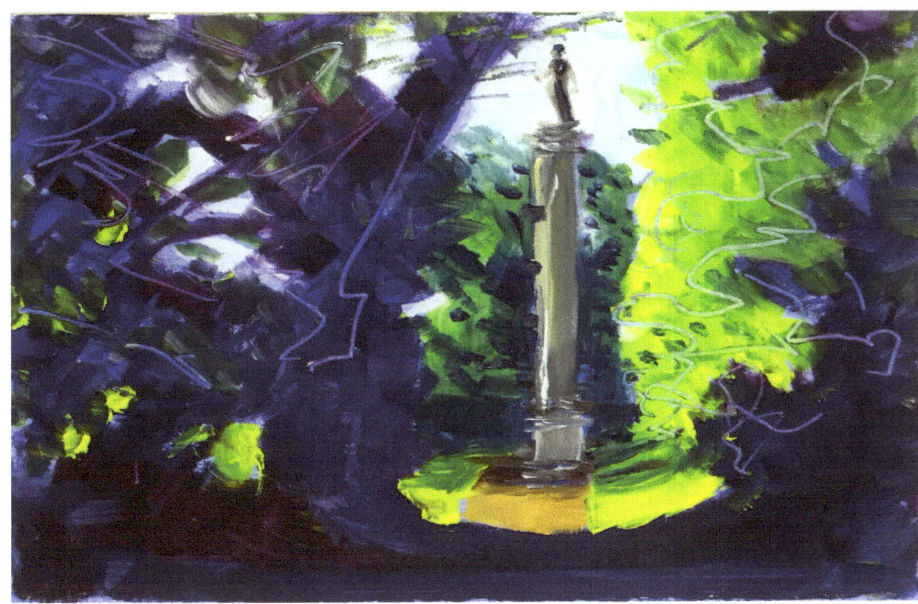

'Captain Grenville's Column'
30th September

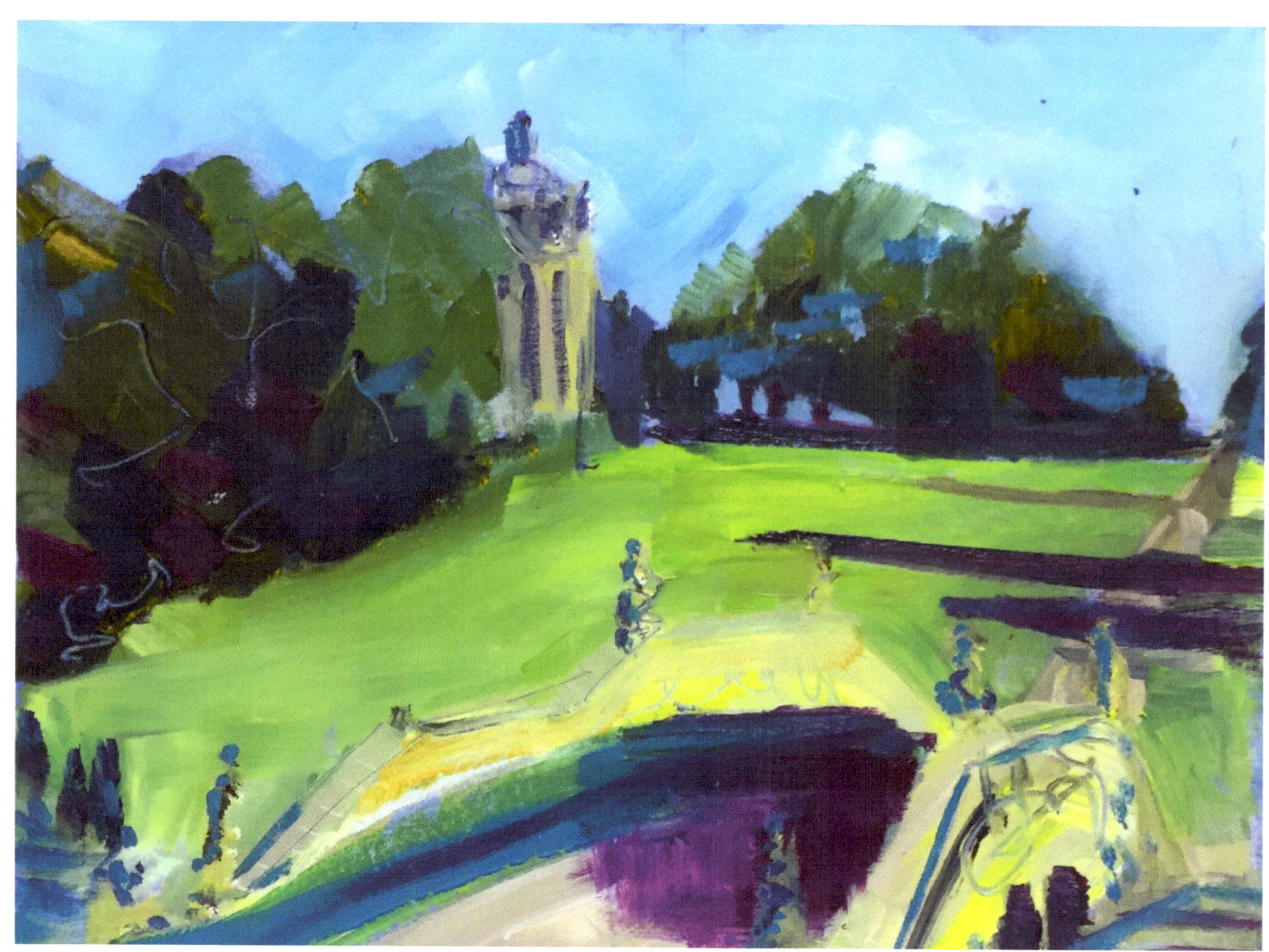

'The Oxford Bridge'
23rd September

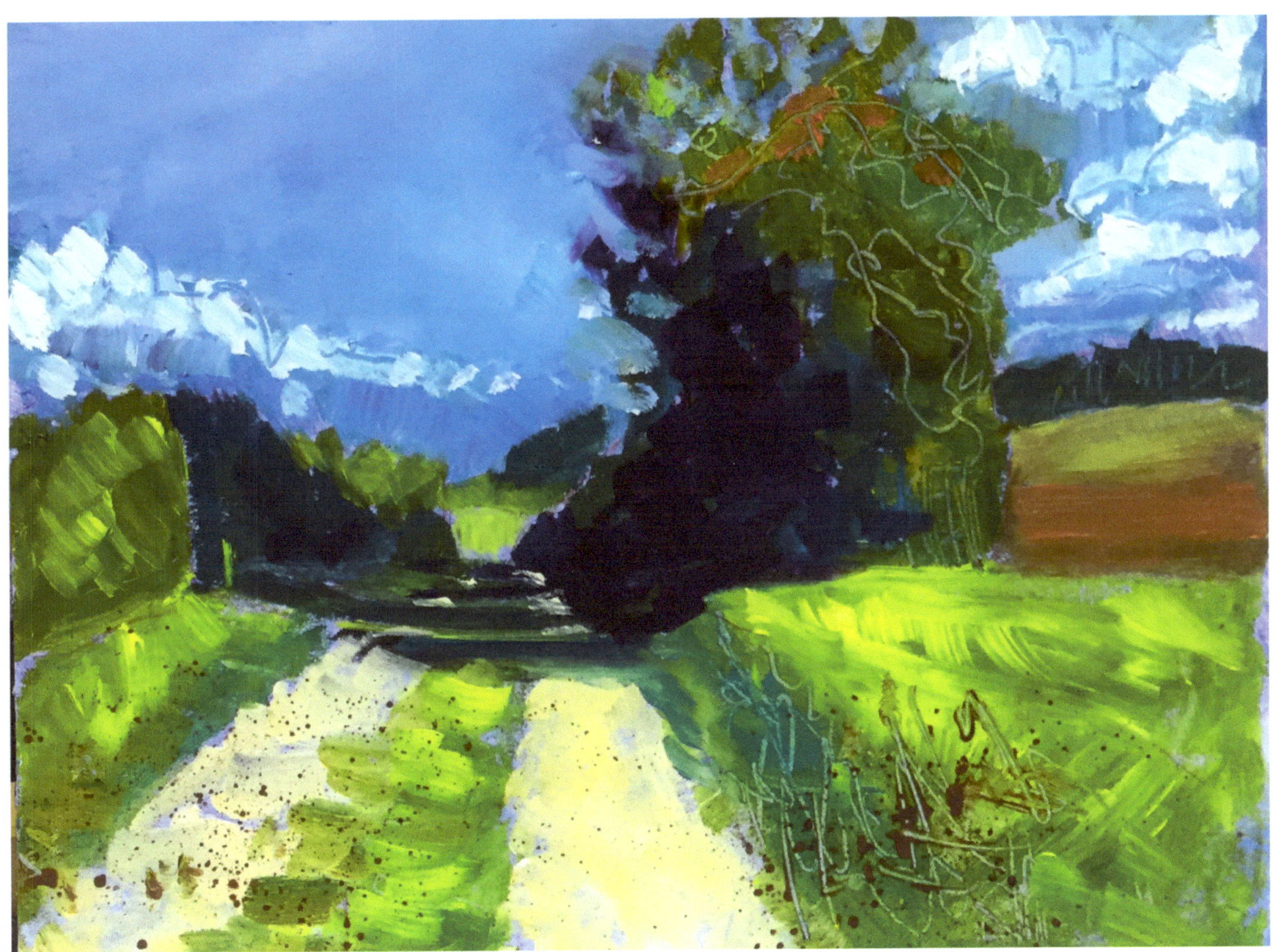

'Walk from Steeple Claydon to Hillesden'
27th September

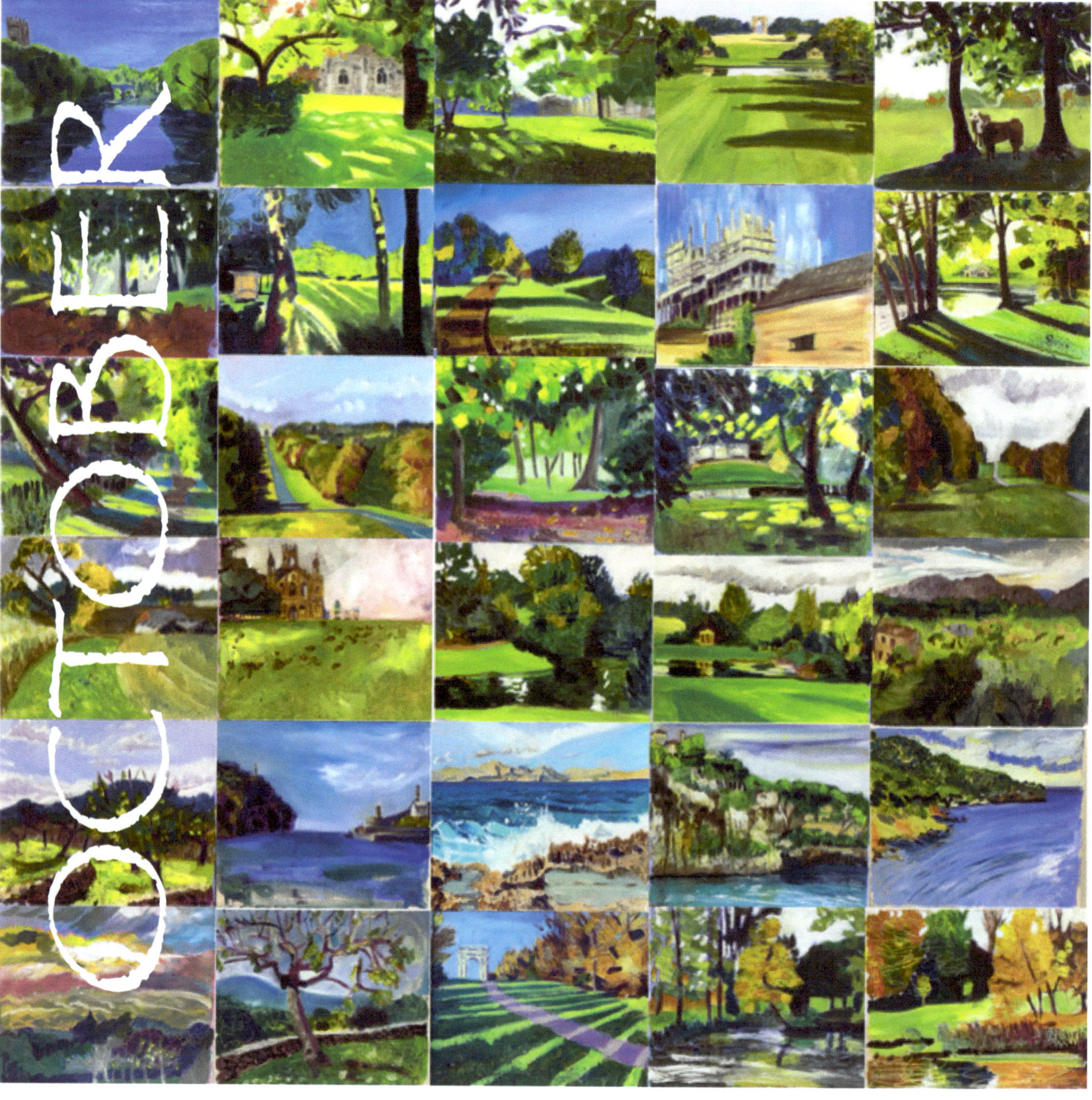
OCTOBER

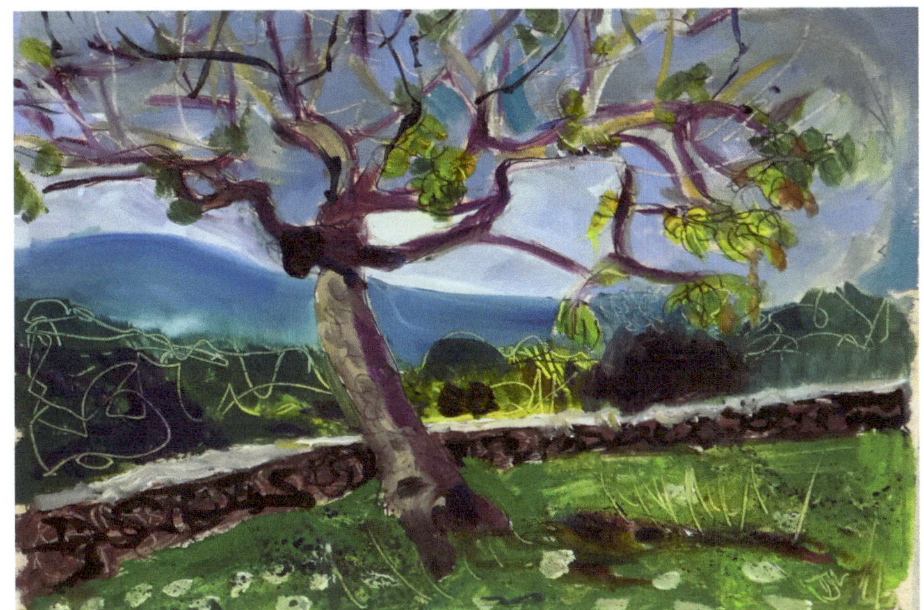

'Fig Tree, Mallorca'
27th October

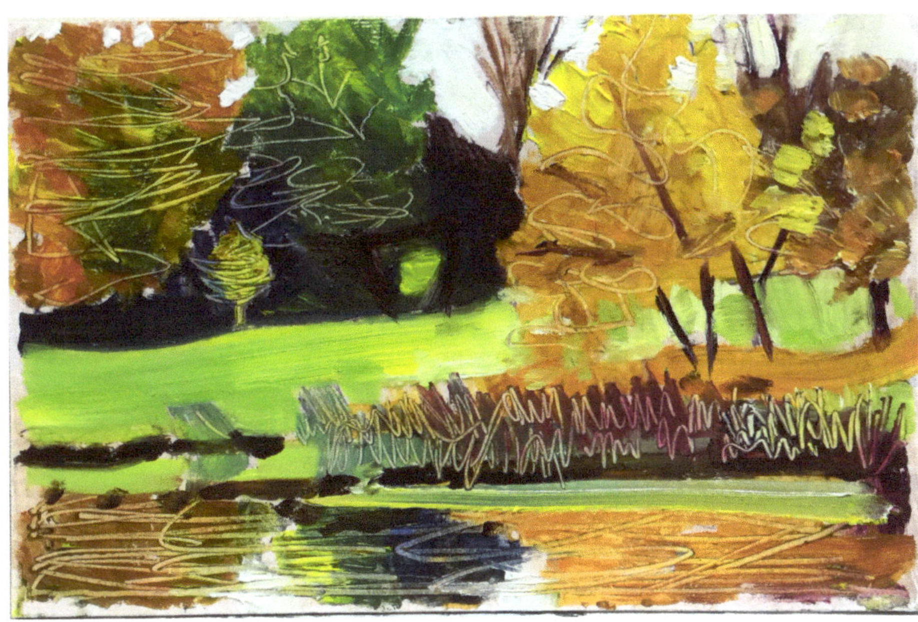

'Towards the Temple of Friendship'
30th October

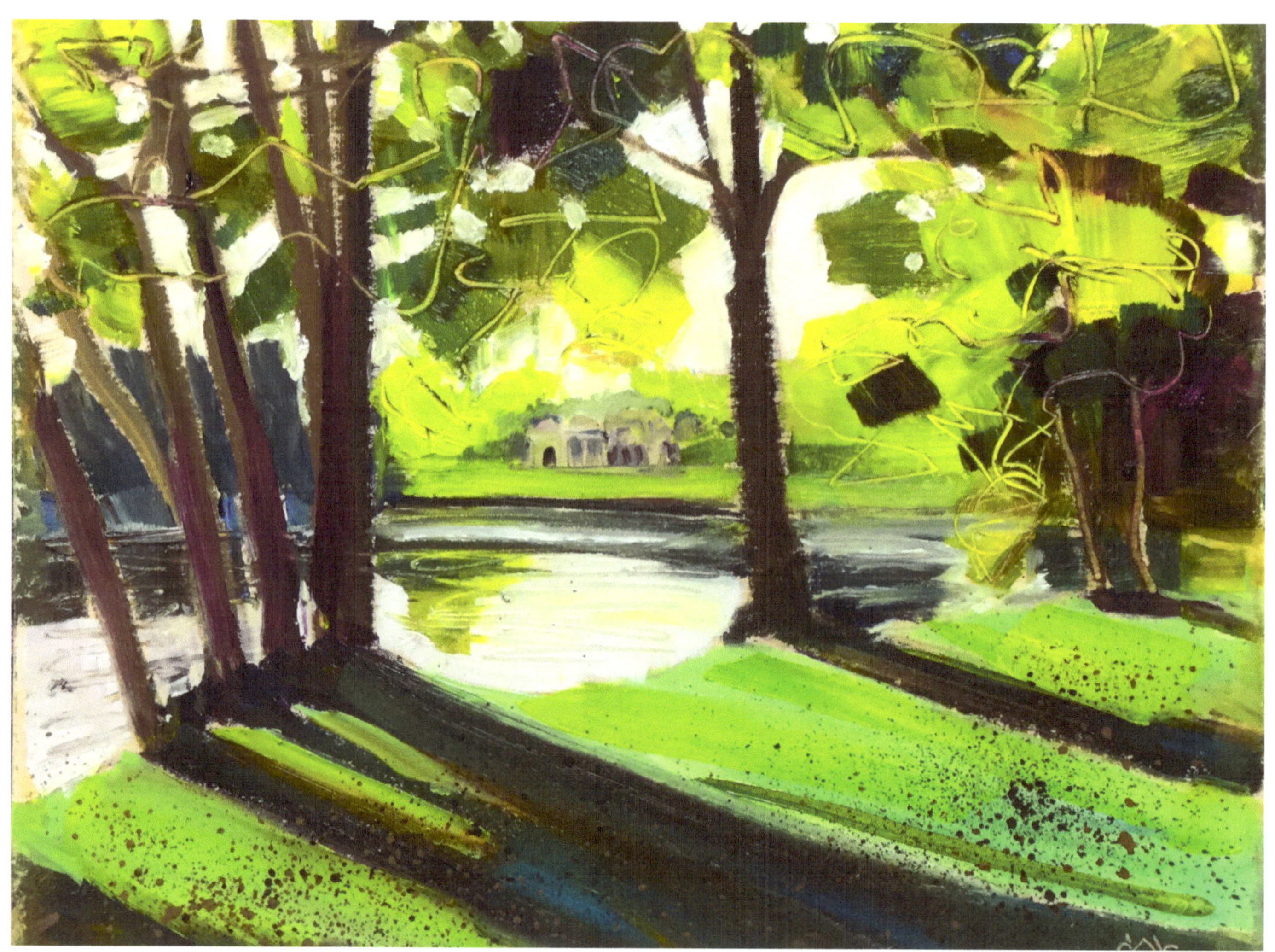

'Eleven Acre Lake glimpsing the Temple of Venus'
10th October

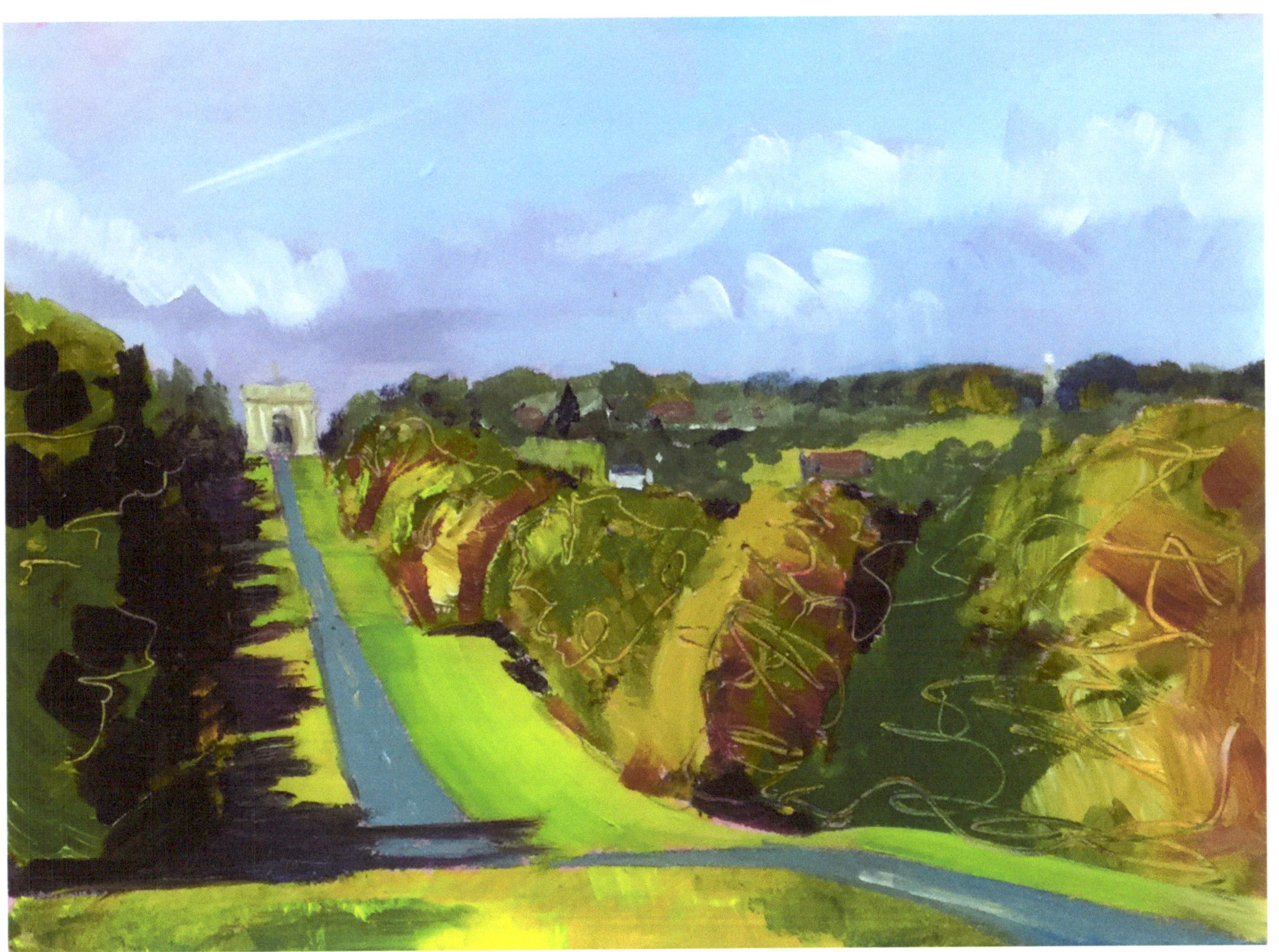

'Stowe Avenue, Autumn Trees'
12th October

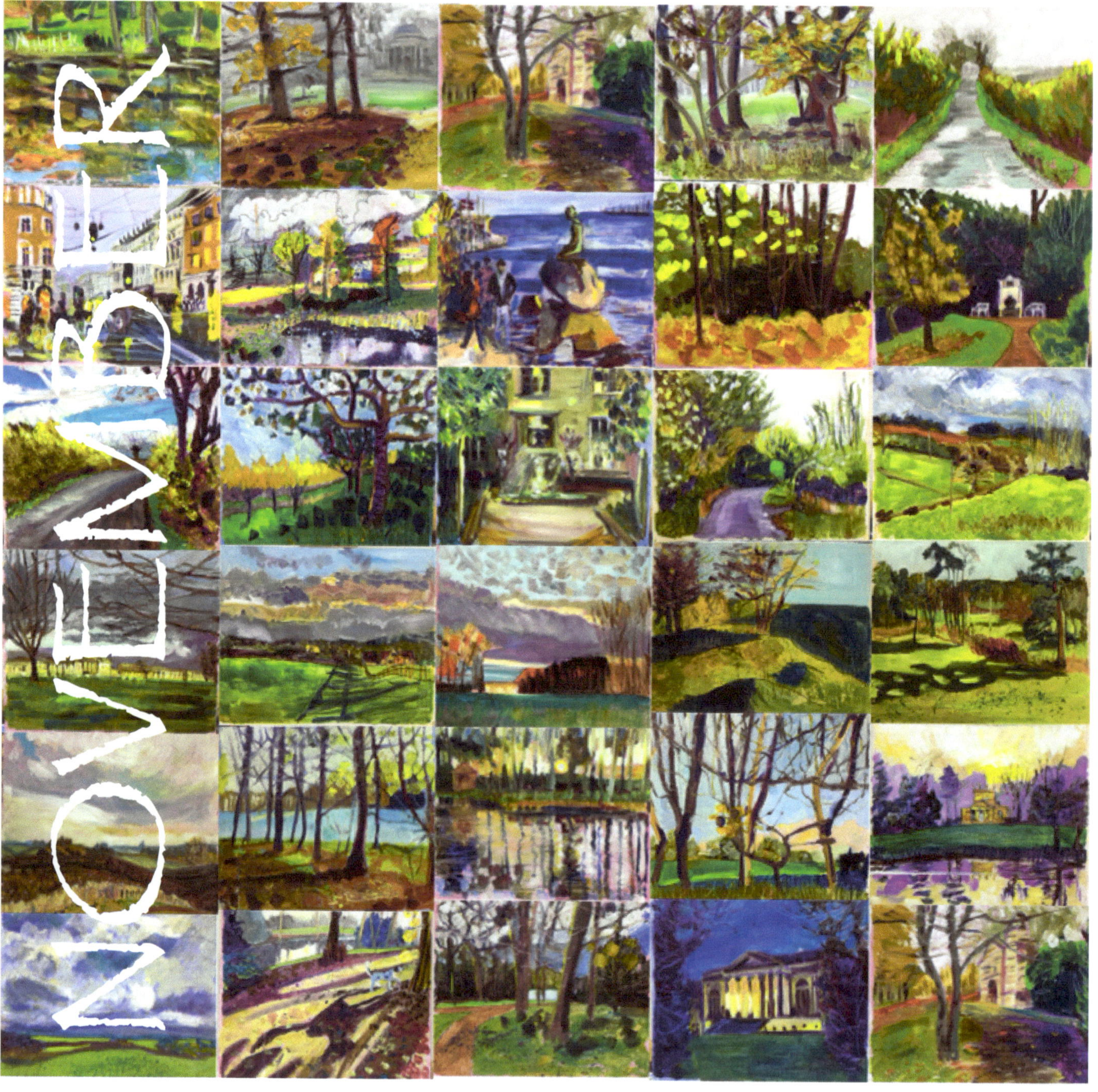
NOVEMBER

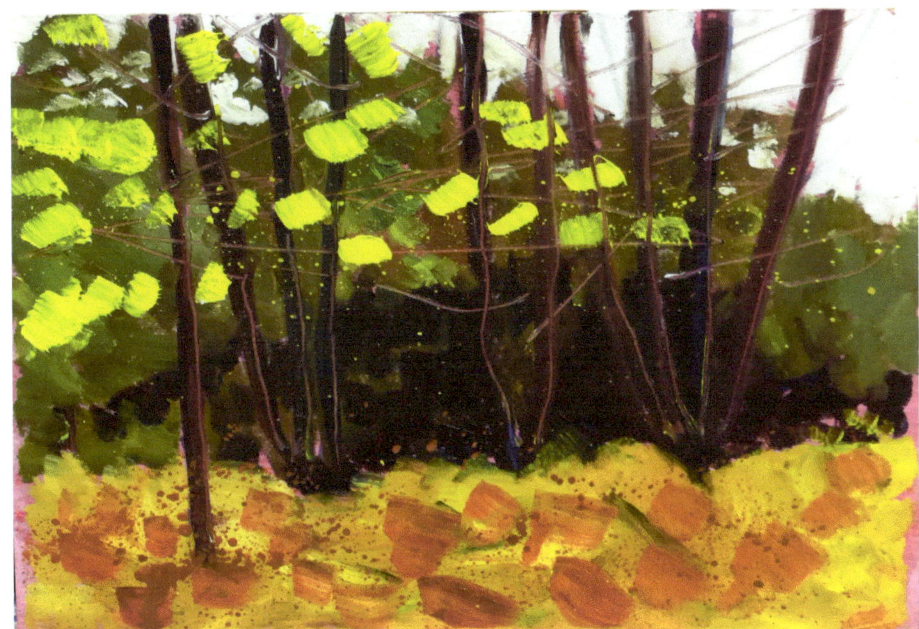

'By the River Styx in the Eylsian Fields'
9th November

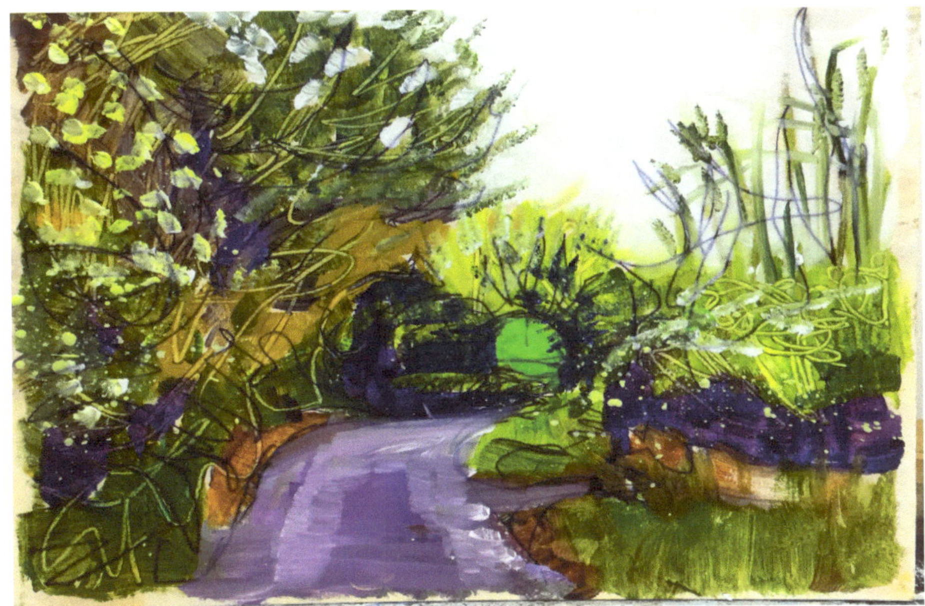

'Foyle Tree Tunnel'
15th November

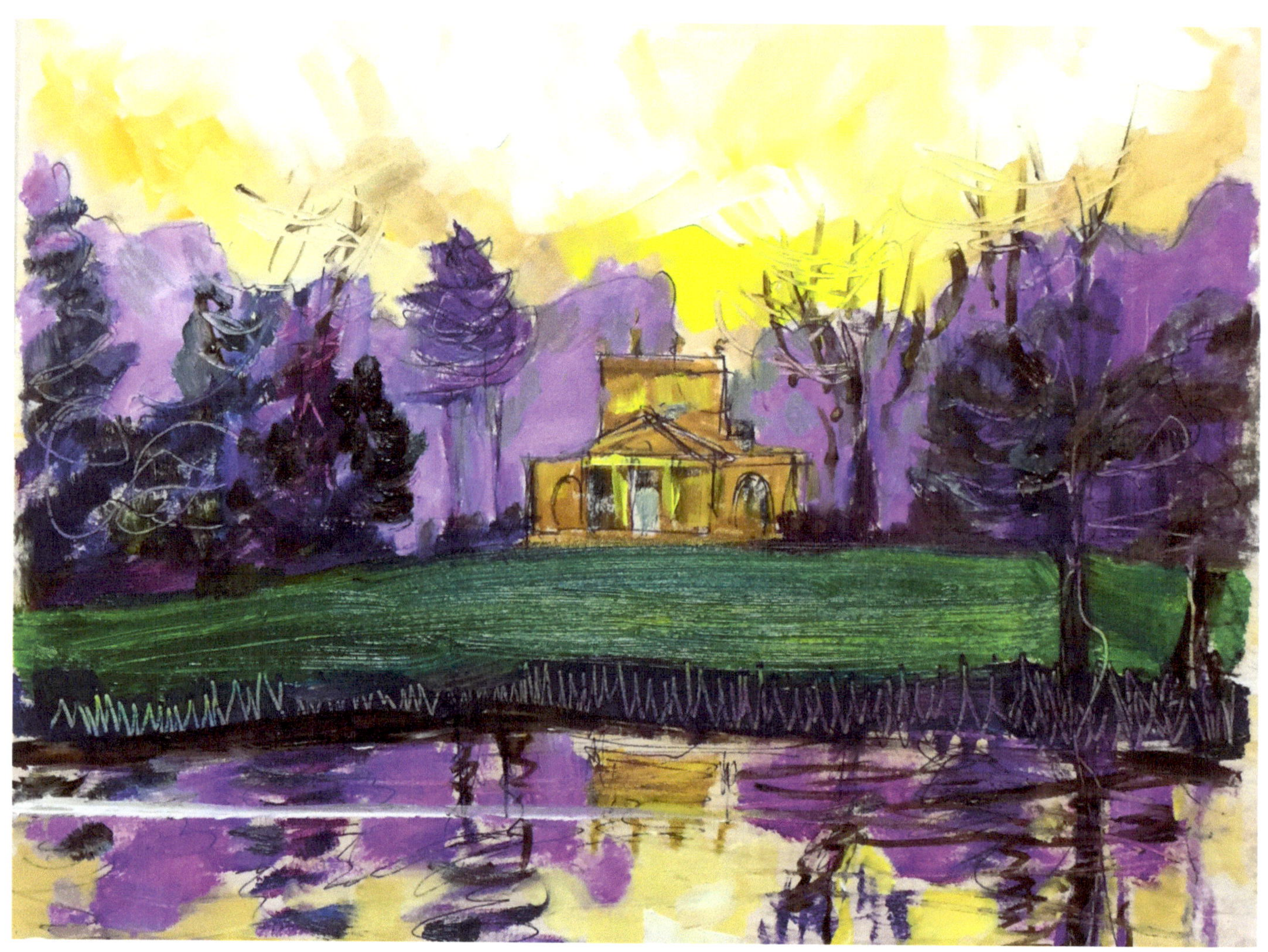

'The Temple of Friendship'
26th November

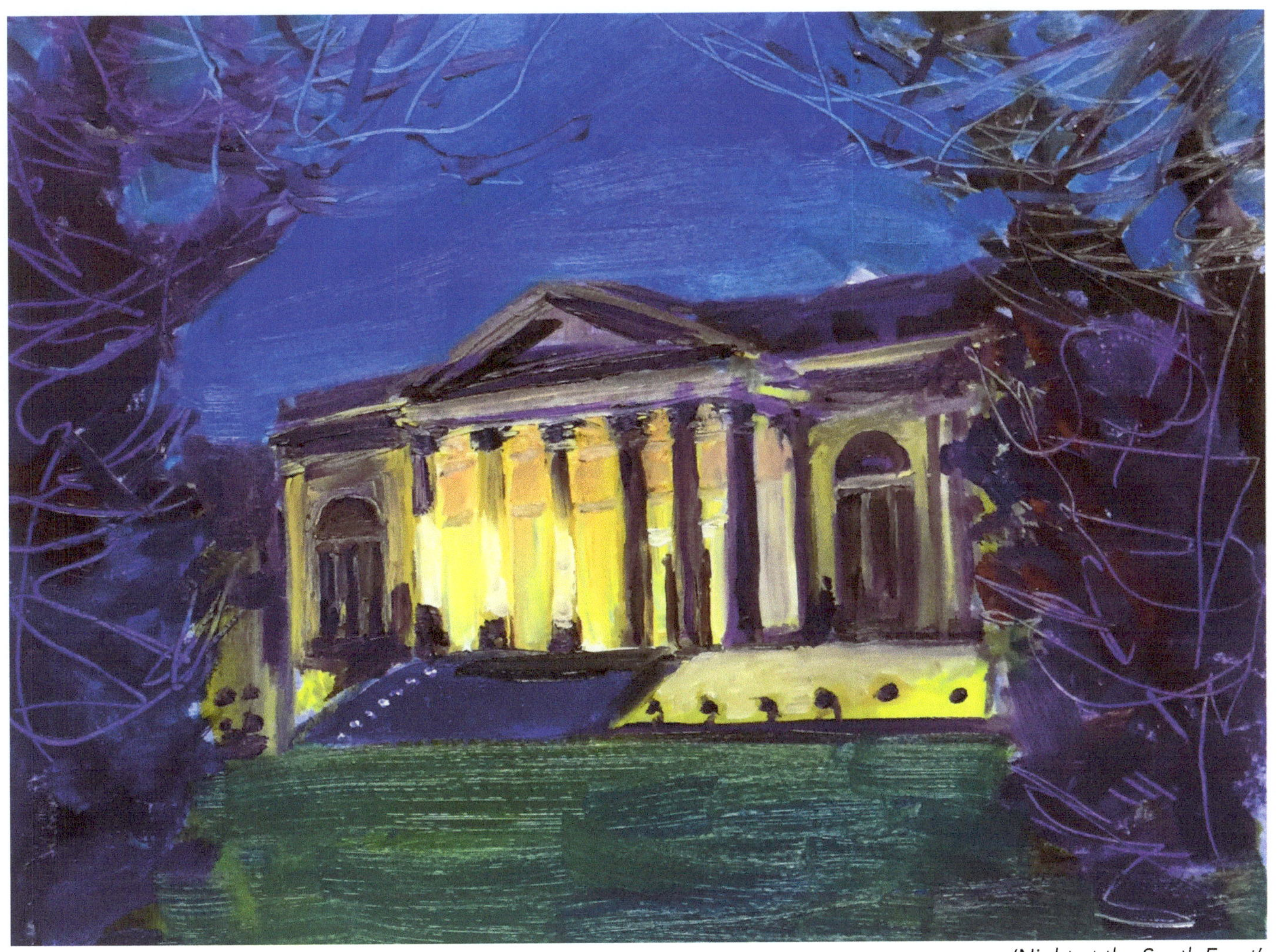

'Night at the South Front'
30th November

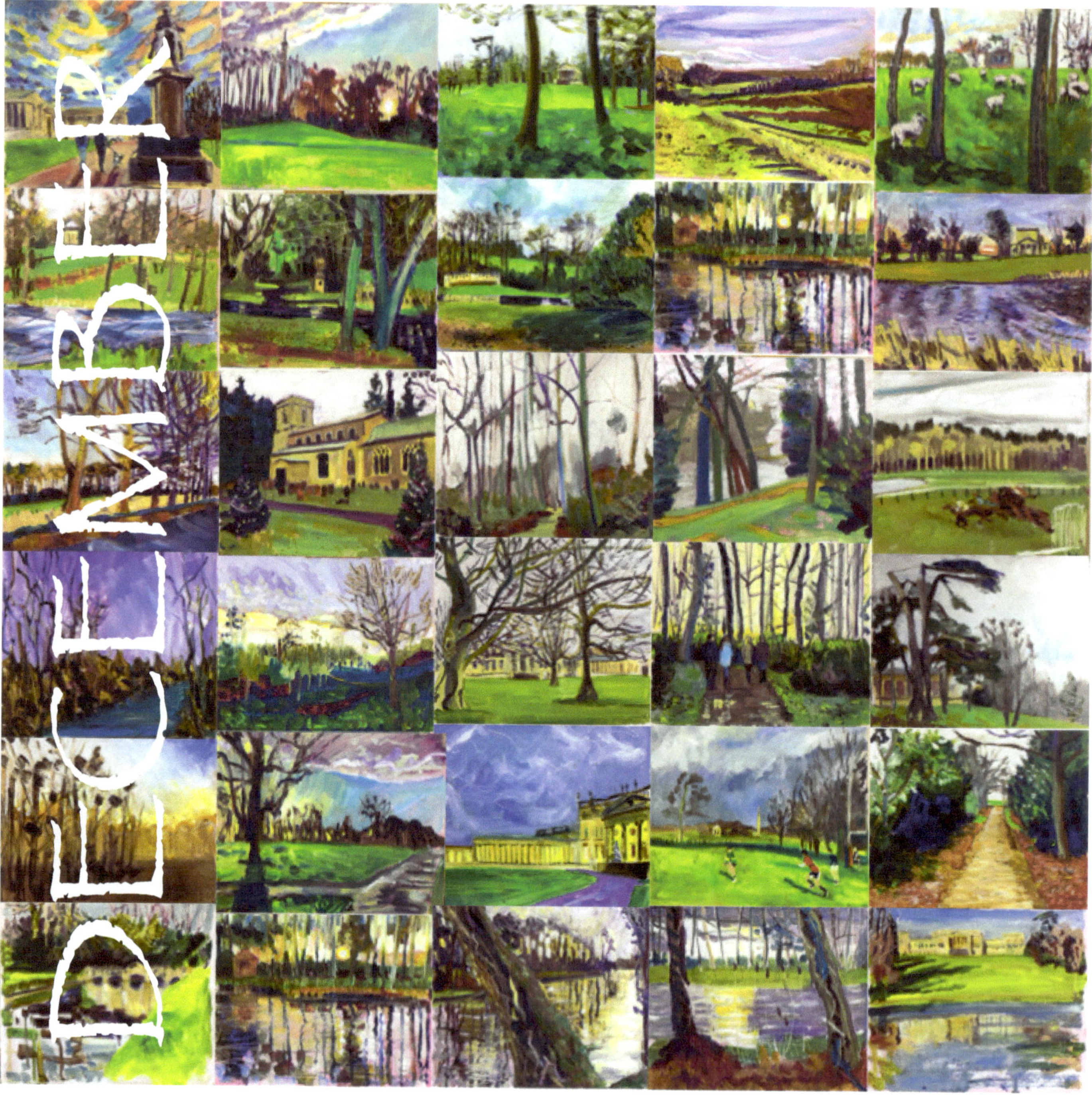
DECEMBER

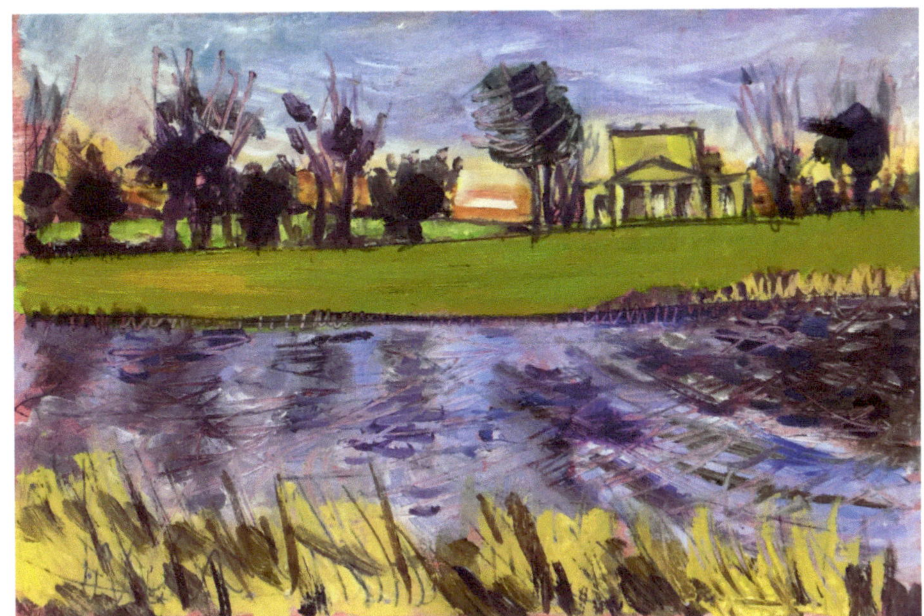

'The Temple of Friendship'
10th December

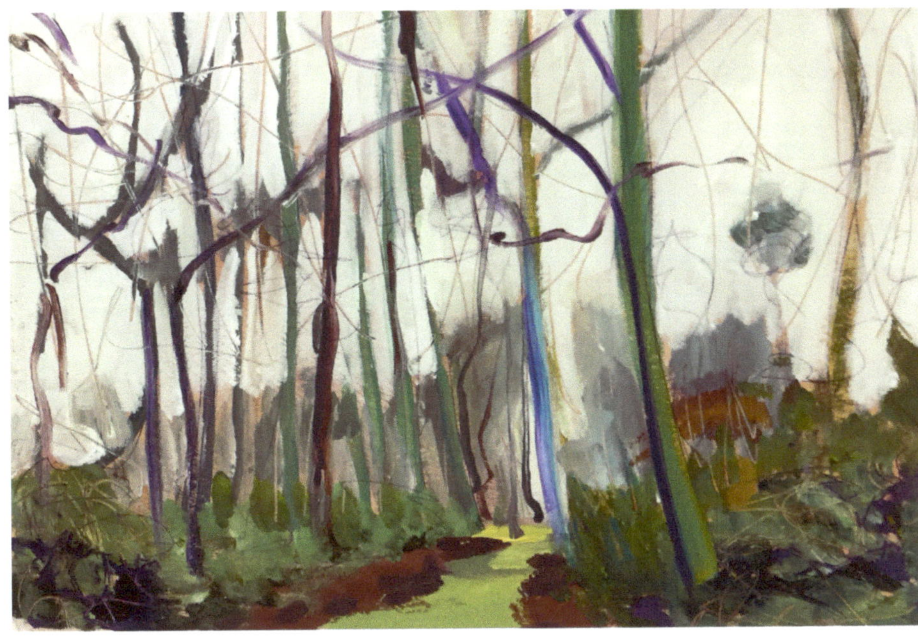

'Grecian Valley, Grass Walk'
13th December

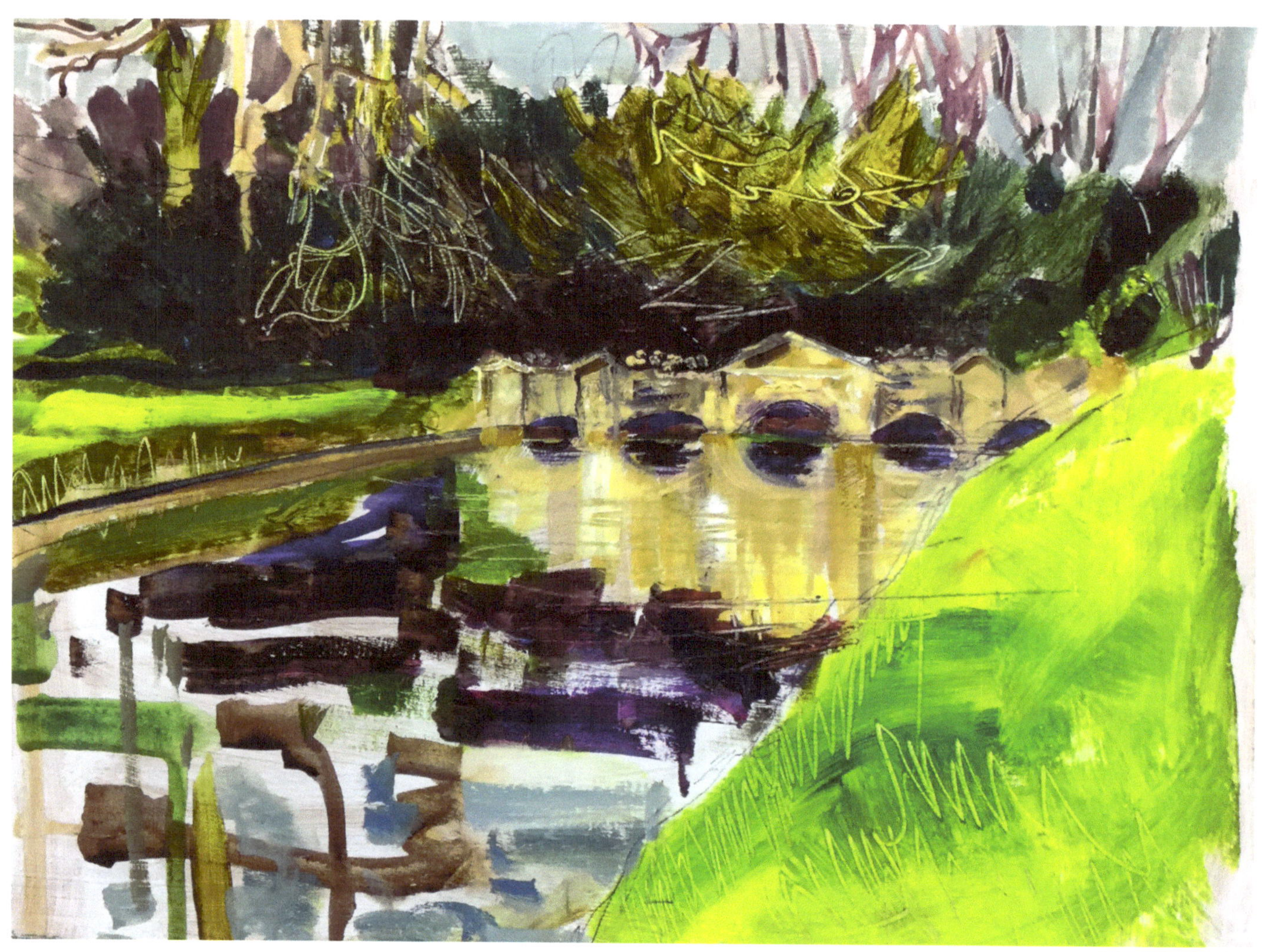

'Shell Bridge'
28th December

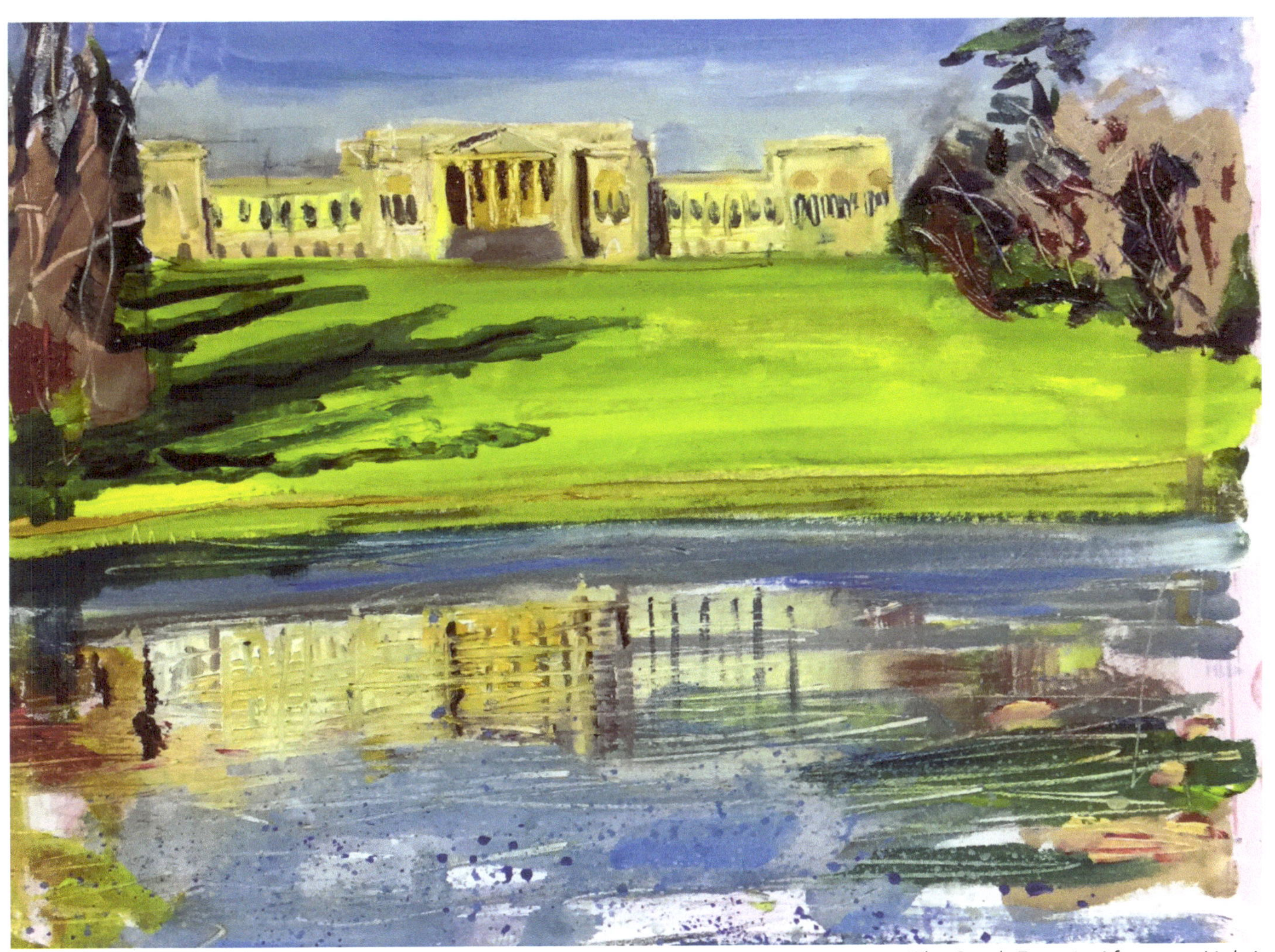

'The South Front in Afternoon Light'
31st December

Deborah Last

Deborah Last works from her studio on the edge of the beautiful Stowe Landscape gardens. She works directly from life and from memory to create light filled work.

Throughout 2015 Deborah explored the landscape in oils, capturing the light and weather of a moment, every day. Her contemporary style of expressive colour and intriguing brush strokes blended with a traditional form of art created a unique and beautiful series of paintings. Undertaking daily painting has further informed Debs' understanding of seasonal light and mood as she observed her favourite locations; The Grecian Valley, The Octagon Lake and the Mansion itself, altering in tone as the year progressed.

This collection of Daily Paintings was exhibited at Stowe House during the Spring/Summer of 2016.

In 2013 Deborah produced the installation piece 'Upper Room' which combines sound, body printing and anatomical drawing. It is a work exploring and examining body image, self-worth and faith.

Having spent 7 years living in India working as an artist and tutor, her work retains the love of colour and story that so inspired her whilst she was there.

Her work is held in private collections throughout the UK and abroad, including Sir Richard FitzHerbert of Tissington Hall, Derbyshire and the estate of Sir Jack Hayward, Barbados.

Together with her fellow artist and friend Zoë Day she owns Buckingham Art School.
She is a Patron and a founding member of Buckingham Art for All.

For sales, commissions or to book a talk, demo or workshop please contact: dlast@btinternet.com or visit Deborah's online shop; www.dlast.tictail.com

www.deborahlast.co.uk
Instagram: debs_last
Facebook: Deborah Last artist.
www.buckinghamartschool.com

Hope For Justice

Deborah is proud to be fundraising for the charity Hope For Justice, who are commited to ending modern-day slavery and human trafficking. When you purchase a painting, or this book from Deborah, 20% of proceeds will go towards preventing atrocities happening here in the UK, and across the world.

Hope For Justice works to train proffessionals to be able to spot those vulnerable people who are being exploited and provide outreach programmes. Their investigators work with police to rescue those affected by human trafficking, and provide them with safe homes and ultimately secure criminal and civil justice for victims.

For more information about this charity, please visit hopeforjustice.org
Hope For Justice is a registered charity No. 1126097 in England & Wales and No. SC045769 in Scotland.

www.ingramcontent.com/pod-product-compliance
Ingram Content Group UK Ltd.
Pitfield, Milton Keynes, MK11 3LW, UK
UKHW060101300726
14090UKWH00003B/340

* 9 7 8 0 9 9 2 8 8 4 2 1 5 *